Malcolm,
Wishing you a very happy birthday
from Andrew, Eunice
Paul, Mark + Nicola.

Vineyards and Vignerons

VINEYARDS
&
VIGNERONS

by
Robin and Judith
Yapp

Printed by Blackmore Press, Shaftesbury, Dorset.

*For
Rowan
Margaret
who was born while
the Muscadet article was
being written and who made
her first journey through the
vineyards of the Loire
at the age of
fifteen
days*

CONTENTS

INTRODUCTION

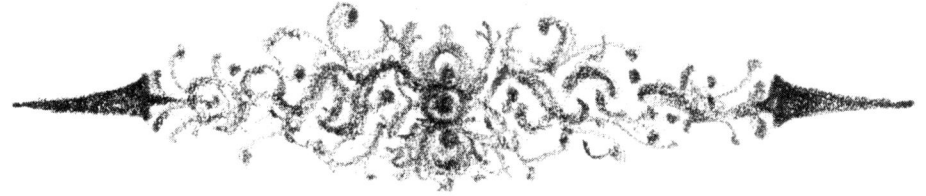

For the past ten years the appearance of the lace-like fronds of cow parsley in the hedgerows around Mere have triggered off a love-hate reaction. Their luxuriant growth signifies the onset of early summer, but to us also indicates that we are woefully behindhand with the writing of our annual wine list. As we are proudly aware that 1979 marks the tenth anniversary of Yapp Brothers, an expanded list was envisaged as a celebratory gesture and preparation was put under way in good time. In the event everything has been completed before even the curly leaves of cow parsley have become visible; we now have an opportunity of relishing the burgeoning of the hedges without the distraction and worry that had begun to seem inevitable. A major surprise to us is that our expanded notes have become a book. We have had the great good fortune that Charles Mozley should have become enamoured of our project; Charles has decorated the pages that follow with charming conceits and good-humoured drawings that could only have emanated from his pencil.

Yapp Brothers was started early in 1969 as a seriously intended business specializing solely in the wines of the Loire and Rhône valleys of France; serious though modest, we realised that we had to learn our new trade as we went along. For four years our store was the garage of Hinckes Mill House, hidden away in the lanes two miles south of Mere. Yapp Brothers prospered, more and more customers were anxious to pay a visit, until the inaccessibility of the house and the appalling lack of storage space enforced an early move. Various highly unsuitable premises were considered until, in a glorious moment of revelation, we realised that we had been passing the ideal, the only, possibility three or four times each day. There, in the middle of Mere, stood the Old Milk Factory, a conglomeration of warehouses, offices, cottages and garden, all falling into a high state of disrepair.

At that time the property "boom" was at its height; the site had been bought by a property company who presumably hoped to use the land for some ambitious and profitable development. Our strong desire to acquire the buildings made us a naive target for the Londoners, but the premium that they extracted from us was well worth paying. The task that lay ahead was the justifiable cause of many a nightmare; to purchase a vast, decaying property is not conducive to easy nights. As it turned out, it was the very dilapidation of the central structure that showed the solution: we employed a bulldozer to drive around in ever increasing circles until only the peripheral buildings remained; the mounds of rubble conveniently served to fill various large holes, and we were left with a large courtyard surrounded by a house, an office and several attractive warehouses.

Our fountain, a copy of the lovely provençal fountain in the centre of Châteauneuf-du-Pape, is the realisation of a nocturnal delusion of grandeur: we were somewhat disconcerted when a London firm of stone masons willingly agreed to carve it, using a photograph of the original as a model. The alarmingly high cost was immediately justified in our minds when the immensely heavy pieces of stone arrived and were laboriously pieced together. That our version is slightly larger and in a rather better state of repair than the one in France is now only a minimal source of embarrassment. The tinkling of water spouting from the grotesque masks (when the recirculating pump is functioning properly) is a soothing accompaniment to a glass of wine taken beneath a coloured parasol that wards off the full heat of the sun—when that too is functioning as it should.

The sixty foot industrial chimney was spared at the time of general demolition as a latter-day folly: it serves no practical purpose, but we think it an attractive monument. Neither can the "Grotto", a curious room where half the floor space is not, but a deep, clear pool instead, be justified by reasons of practicality, unless we were to use the icy cold spring water to cool bottles of wine, as churns of milk used to be kept fresh before being taken to the station at Gillingham by horse and cart, to be put on the evening train to London.

Particular excitement was generated when we discovered that, in a period prior to the seventy year use as a milk depot, the three sixteenth and seventeenth century cottages that now form part of our house had been the Town Brewery. Two brothers named Lander had a thriving enterprise until the temperance movement swept the south-west of England. With a degree of imagination that we would wish to emulate if catastrophe ever threatens us, the Lander boys reviewed their diminishing sales and presented themselves at the next Temperance meeting as converts to the cause, announcing later that their establishment would be open for business the following week as a retail source of bacon, eggs and cheese.

Our ten years as Wine Merchants have been highly educative and extremely enjoyable. Of all the pleasant things that we have experienced in that time, none has been more rewarding than our encounters with the men who make the wines we sell, the *vignerons*. If we have been to some degree able to evoke their lives, homes, habits and the wines that they so lovingly create, our purpose will have been amply fulfilled.

Robin and Judith Yapp   *The Old Brewery,*
                                           Mere, Wiltshire
                                           May 1979

RIVER LOIRE & ITS TRIBUTARIES

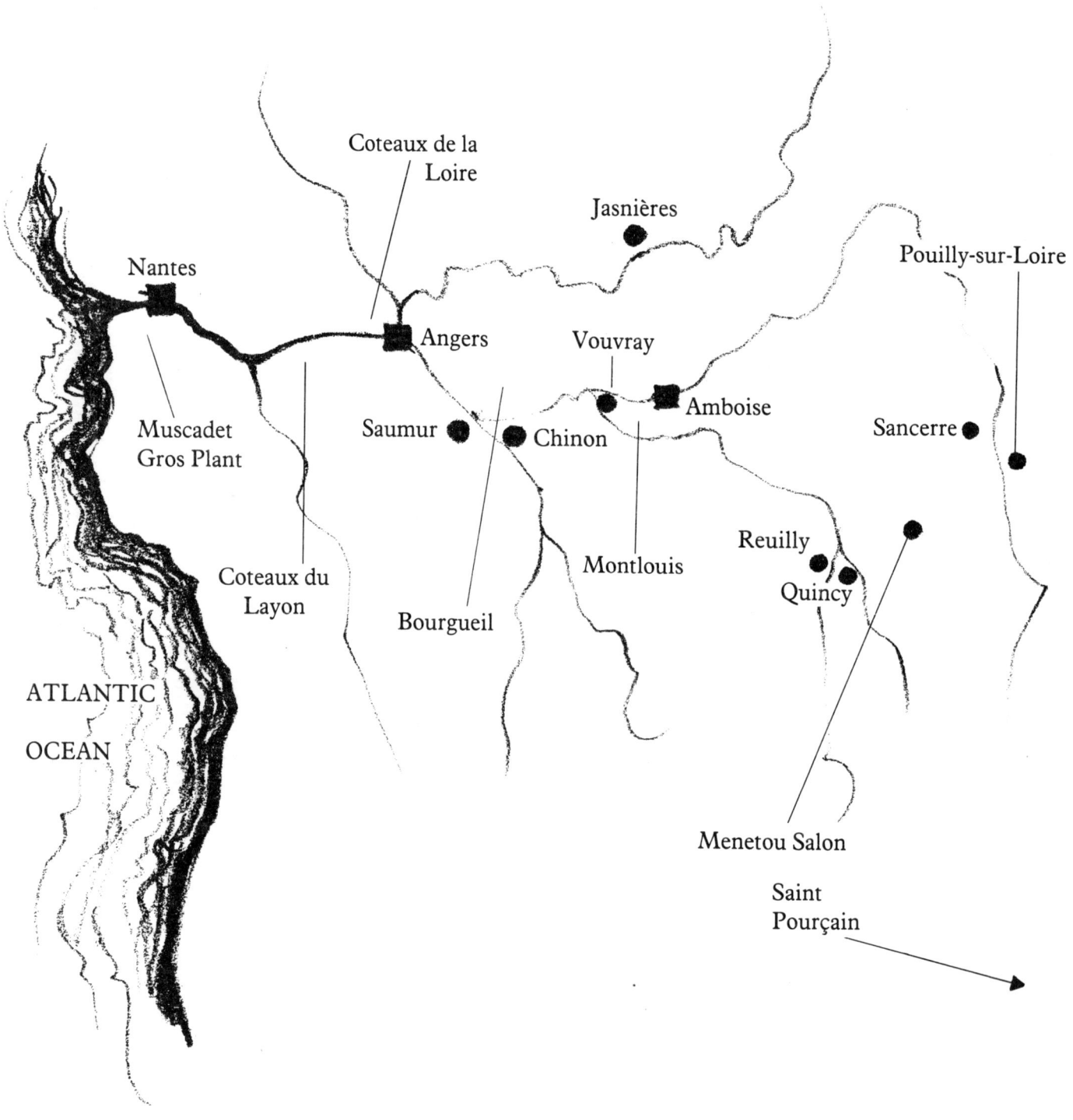

Coteaux de la Loire

Jasnières

Pouilly-sur-Loire

Nantes

Vouvray

Muscadet Gros Plant

Saumur

Chinon

Amboise

Sancerre

Coteaux du Layon

Bourgueil

Montlouis

Reuilly

Quincy

ATLANTIC

OCEAN

Menetou Salon

Saint Pourçain

Angers

LOIRE

MUSCADET-SUR-LIE

It is nigh on incredible to imagine that Muscadet, now one of the best-known wines of all and ubiquitously available, could ever have ranked as a "discovery." Yet as recently as forty years ago, Muscadet was virtually unknown outside the immediate area of its production. As in the case of Sancerre fifteen or twenty years later, the wine gradually became fashionable in the bars and *brasseries* of Paris and from thence permeated the world.

Muscadet is made over a large area to the south, south-west and west of Nantes, the last city on the Loire before it joins the Atlantic. The region is densely planted; in places vineyards stretch in all directions as far as the eye can see. The vine, the *muscadet*, or *melon de bourgogne*, starts to fruit at an early age and is then prolific for twenty years or more, yielding as much as seventy hectolitres per hectare. Thus, a veritable ocean of Muscadet is made, sold and avidly consumed. Unfortunately, most reflective drinkers will remember encounters with so-called Muscadets that gave no pleasure at all, that were in fact down-right nasty. The enormous world thirst for Muscadet has often led to its "stretching" with an inferior, cheaper wine; in some cases there has been downright fraudulent substitution. Henri Bour, of Domaine de Grangeneuve in the Tricastin, recalls the days when white wine—of fair quality, he hastens to add—was dispatched from his estates in Algeria to the Atlantic port of La Rochelle, where he well knew it would be re-christened as Muscadet.

A genuine Muscadet is a robust, patently honest, reassuring sort of wine; well-made, it is full, fruity, eminently quaffable and the ideal accompaniment to the *fruits de mer* of the Brittany coast. The initial taste of such a Muscadet can be quite a revelation. We first met the Chéreau wine at the delightfully peaceful hidden away *Auberge de la Cascade* at Clisson, in the middle of Sèvre-et-Maine, itself reputedly the best of the sub-divisions of the Muscadet region. Previous explorations through Sèvre-et-Maine had revealed undoubted Muscadets, very acceptable wines. Here, at the water's edge beside an old water mill, its machinery whirring, we had at last achieved our ambition, to find a truly fine Muscadet.

Although only five kilometres away, the cluster of cottages of Le Village Boucher proved to be most elusive. We had made numerous false turns and had endured the ignominy of being towed out of a vineyard ditch by a towering, vine-striding tractor before we finally located the Chéreau house. We often wonder when the Chéreaux actually do their vineyard work; on this first occasion, as on all those subsequent, they were in their tiny, sand-floored cellar. Henri, wearing tartan slippers, a brown gauloise adhering to his lower lip, was leaning against a barrel, pipette in one hand, a glass in the other. His father, Étienne, was debating the nuances of the contents of a dozen small barrels with several neighbours, reminiscing of former vintages. On one wall, an ancient wooden carving of Saint Vincent, patron saint of *vignerons*, serenely contemplated a luridly coloured plaster gnome opposite, the gnome condemned to pour Muscadet eternally from a plaster bottle clutched in both arms.

Henri and Étienne are so steeped in wine-making that we doubt they could make an inferior wine if they tried. It is precisely because they use the methods practised by generations of Chéreaux before them—traditional, peasant methods, that their Muscadet is so very, very good. Elsewhere a wine is racked from barrel to barrel and filtered to remove it from the sediment of the products of fermentation. All is then safe, the wine clear, and bottling is easy. Henri and Étienne take risks, but only because they know that thus they can produce a far better wine. The barrels remain untouched from vintage time until the following Spring,

[17]

the wine in permanent contact with the lees, or *lie*. Bottling from off the sediment is tricky and nerve-racking; one false move, one air-lock, and the lees would be disturbed, to cloud the wine and lead to an unpleasant secondary fermentation in bottle. Carefully and skilfully done as by Chéreau *père et fils*, no errors occur, and the wine is bottled crystal-clear. The gain is enormous, and worth all the effort. Muscadet-sur-lie is altogether more interesting, more characterful and fruitier than wines made more commercially.

There are hazards in having dealings with peasant growers. Henri Chéreau is kind natured and straightforward; he is also obstinate. Try as we would, we could not convince him that any other method of vinification exists and that *sur lie* on the label would be beneficial. Finally, we had appropriately worded labels printed in England. We can be as prudent as French peasant growers, which is very cautious indeed. Henri would never take advantage, we are certain, but somehow we have never told him that our initial printing was enormous and that we have labels for years to come. Negotiations over price just might be affected if he realised the degree of our commitment to his lovely wine. The *millésimes*, vintage labels, or the lack of them, proved to be another hurdle. A great uncle had bequeathed to Henri about a million neck labels reading "Grande Réserve", and thereafter his sense of economy precluded a printing of labels indicating the vintage. British wine consumers appear to be less convinced by resonant slogans than the French; eventually we had to have vintage labels printed ourselves. Perhaps Henri has passed the "Grande Réserve" on to a nephew: he certainly will not have destroyed them.

GROS PLANT

Every Muscadet grower makes an even drier white wine called Gros Plant. Gros Plant falls into the classification below that of *appellation contrôlée*; it is V.D.Q.S., *Vin Délimité de Qualité Supérieure*. The vine is the *folle blanche*, grown in the Charentais to produce the thin, acidic wine from which Cognac is distilled. The Loire wine is far more potable, though undoubtedly dry; indeed, it is eye-screwingly dry. We would not care for Gros Plant as a daily beverage, but on occasion, especially in summer, it is the tipple for which Yapp taste buds crave, and then no other wine will touch the spot. Another tremendous justification for the existence of Gros Plant is its perfect suitability as the partner of Crème de Cassis in a Kir.

MALVOISIE

Saint Geréon, a village to the west of Ancenis, marks the north-eastern bounds of Muscadet production, and the wine made there, Coteaux de la Loire, is supposedly only marginally inferior to that of Sèvre-et-Maine. Jacques Guindon is a burly, genial man whose Coteaux de la Loire is particularly esteemed. We sought him out, not for his Muscadet, but because he is of the last few *vignerons* still making an unusual light red wine and a *rosé* from the *gamay Beaujolais*. Coteaux d'Ancenis has V.D.Q.S. status. It is curious that so little is made as the wine is most pleasant. M.Guindon's knowledge of his area is encyclopedic, and he could not have been more helpfully explanatory. Better, he was prepared to let us have a modest quantity of Coteaux d'Ancenis.

On our next visit, we paid more attention to the many certificates and diplomas with which one wall of the cellar is papered. Dating from the end of the last century onwards, they make an impressive display. Our eyes were caught by one in particular, detailing the award of a gold medal in 1926 to a wine of which we had never heard—Malvoisie. Jacques Guindon was amused by our interest and questions. Yes, he still makes a minute quantity, although his few *malvoisie* vines are kept from sentiment rather than reasons of commerce. The same grape appears elsewhere in France under a variety of names. Known in Alsace as *tokay* and as *fromentot* in Champagne, it is the very same grape as *pinot gris*, the *cépage* of one of our favourite *rosés*, Pinot Gris, of Reuilly.

The name Malvoisie is thought to derive from the ancient city of Malvasia in the Pelopennese. During the Middle Ages and earlier, all the trade routes of Asia Minor passed through Malvasia. How the vine and its name came to this particular corner of France remains a mystery, but the *malmsey* grape of Madeira is said to share the same origin. It would be interesting and instructive to compare the two, in order to establish whether or not they are identical.

We are delighted that Kenneth Bell, M.B.E., includes a few of our wines on the list of his celebrated restaurant, Thornbury Castle, but what gives us particular pleasure is the presence there of Malvoisie. It was at Thornbury Castle, on Saturday 25th December 1507, that "Ninety-five gentry, one hundred and seven yeomen and ninety-seven garcons" sat down with the third Duke of Buckingham to celebrate the Feast of the Nativity. An amazing and daunting variety of meats and game was washed down with "eleven pottles and three quarts of Gascony wine, price 13s, one and a half pitchers of Rhenish wine, price 15d, half pitcher Malvoisey, price 6d."

It is impossible to imagine what the Malvoisie of those days was like, or how potable. Jacques Guindon's version is very special and fast becoming a favourite with our customers. The pale-straw colour and the rich, sweetish taste are immediately likeable, indeed ingratiating, but it is the extraordinary spectrum of flavour that strongly indicates the enhancement that bottle-age may bring. The only sad thing is that "pottles and pitchers" cost more than sixpence a time nowadays.

[21]

SAVENNIÈRES

The wines of Savennières are so particular and so pleasing that we have long expected them to gain high popularity in Britain. Certainly Savennières has found some favour since the start of our proselytizing ten years ago, but ours has been a small, individual campaign; it is naive to have hoped for speedier results.

The vineyards lie in a semi-circle around the small town of Savennières, on the north bank of the Loire, ten kilometres south west of Angers. Here the *chenin blanc* produces wines markedly different from the far better-known Vouvrays and Montlouis of Touraine. Here in Anjou the wines are predominantly dry, full bodied, fleshy, almost chewy, with a crisp, apple-like tang.

The cellars of Domaine de la Bizolière are in Savennières itself, hidden away among the back streets of stone cottages. The cellars are so unpretentious as to be difficult to recognise, even when located. The day to day running of the establishment is in the capable hands of Albert Giraud, a quiet, gentle, slow-speaking man. In the small office, his wife is likely to be hand gumming labels and affixing them to bottles. The *chai* is a long, low, cool, dark hall with several hundred small barrels in neat, ordered rows on the earth floor. Albert flourishes his pipette and proceeds to remove the glass bung from keg after keg; a tasting at Bizolière is a daunting marathon.

The Brincard vineyards are north of the town, beside the white wedding cake Belle Époque château of Bizolière, set in a spacious "English" park. Each section of vineyard, *clos,* differs in the constitution of its soil and degree of protection from the elements. Although discernible, the varying nuances of the various wines are difficult, nearly impossible, to describe. The largest volume is of Bizolière itself; with its firm, supple character, Bizolière represents the archetypal Savennières. Clos des Fougeraies is Bizolière surplus to permitted *appellation* quantity. Although identical to Bizolière, it has to be classified as *appellation* Anjou. There is far less made of the finer wines, La Roche aux Moines and Clos du Papillon. In years of disastrous late spring frosts, such as 1977, virtually none is made at all, and M. Giraud wears a long face.

Marc Brincard, the proprietor of Bizolière, is a Baron, but does not care to use his title. He is a banker by profession, spending most of the year in Paris. Several years elapsed before a visit to Savennières coincided with his being in residence. We were subjected to a double surprise: Marc was not the elderly grey-bearded Baron of our imagination, but a slight, boyish young man of great charm. Furthermore, having been educated at Beaumont College and Peterhouse, Cambridge, his English was perfect, far transcending our command of his language.

Last year Marc honoured us by producing two bottles of ancient

lineage, emanating from two small pieces of vineyard that fell into disuse before the last war, Clos de Roussel 1928 and Clos de Malabris 1926. We sat in the elegant salon, reclining in Napoleonic armchairs (M. Giraud in his socks: when invited into the château during working hours, his vineyard boots are left at the door), as Marc delicately poured the precious liquor. The long years in bottle had produced a remarkable transformation; the vibrancy of youth had passed away to leave a soft, dark richness with an almost sherry-like taste.

The sparkling Bizolière is a new venture that has proved highly successful. At vintage time the fresh pressed juice is taken from Savennières to the highly expert firm of Langlois-Château, near Saumur, where it is transformed into *mousseux* by the *méthode champenoise*.

Château de Chamboureau stands amidst its vines near the village of Epiré. In fact, the Soulez' house is a *manoir*, more domestic and less formal than a château, but the conical turrets, the symmetric pavilions to either side of the main dwelling, and the grotesque gargoyles that surmount the gutters betray its feudal origins.

In the centre of the village, Château d'Epiré is protected from the public gaze by high walls. Built at the same time as Bizolière, the most curious feature is the medieval church behind the house. Our first visit to Epiré was during a thunderstorm; the Bizards' housekeeper insisted on taking us to view the church through the downpour, our protests notwithstanding. We were astonished when her purpose was revealed. Since 1900 the church has been the cellar of the château; in place of pews stand serried ranks of barrels, the officiant is the rotund, jolly Friar Tuck-like caviste, Robert Daguin. Epiré is a rather fuller type of Savennières than others; in the better years a small quantity of sweet wine, *moelleux*, is made, as in the days of M. Bizard's father, to please the few octogenarian clients who prefer the old-style wine.

The vines of Domaine du Closel are north of Savennières, but the cellars are at Château de Savennières, hard by the old church. The park is somewhat neglected; a crumbling cast-iron bridge spans a tiny branch of the Loire that regularly floods in spring. Madame de Jessey is seldom at the château, so the visitor has to cope with her intense, sibilant major domo, black-coated Monsieur Villessot. The neat cellar is under the care of a *maître de chai* who is brother-in-law to Giraud of Bizolière, and has the same degree of skill. Several years had elapsed before we realised that M. Cholet and Albert were related. In that time we had gained a quite undeserved reputation as world economists, having reduced our annual orders drastically just before the recession of the early 1970's began to bite deeply. What had been mere commonsense had obviously been discussed often and at length by the two men in the one bar of Savennières. Ever since, our requirements have been looked upon as a barometer of future world finance.

The most famous wine of Savennières is Coulée de Serrant. The vineyard and château were purchased by Madame Joly twenty years ago. A diminutive, dynamic blonde, she has pursued a policy of excellence to such an extent that the standing of Coulée de Serrant, reputed for a century and more, has never been higher. The wine is kept in bottle at the château for at least two years before it is released for sale. This sort of painstaking care, together with Madame Joly's flair for public relations, ensures that Coulée fetches a higher price than its peers. The keen amateur of wine will find it necessary to have a bottle or two in his cellar, but the other fine Savennières, such as La Roche aux Moines or Clos du Papillon probably represent a better buy for general consumption.

For several years there was no Coulée de Serrant to spare for Yapp Brothers or their customers. The timely gift of a dozen enlargements of evocative photographs of the 1972 vintage at Coulée, showing a wooden sledge laden with grape-filled tubs being towed through the luxuriant vines by an old horse, against a background of the Loire, evidently pleased Madame Joly. The following year we received an allocation of the wine.

Bizolière, Closel and Serrant make distinguished, elegant red wines from the *cabernet franc*. As with so many other red wines, they repay the patience required to give them bottle age. After five or six years, the characteristic "lead pencil" taste of *cabernet* softens and ripens into a broad band of satisfyingly related elements.

COTEAUX DU LAYON

Immediately south of Savennières and the Loire, in a region of gently rolling hills and small, hidden valleys, some of the greatest dessert wines of France are produced from the *chenin blanc*. The generic *appellation* of the vineyards that border the small, meandering river Layon is Coteaux du Layon. A large volume of this pleasant *demi-sec* to sweet wine is made. Better favoured slopes with the more individual rating of Chaume consistently produce sweet *moelleux* wines. The most extraordinary wines of the region are Quarts de Chaume and Bonnezeaux, which are always in short supply.

Searching out the vineyards of Quarts de Chaume is far from easy; they lie concealed to the south of Rochefort-sur-Loire. Head for the tall radio mast on the skyline and you will be getting warm. There are only four proprietors of these valuable, steeply slanting slopes; Pascal Laffourcade and his family own the greatest proportion with their two properties, Suronde and Écharderie. The vines are so well protected from the capricious whims of nature that the grapes can ripen fully and become saturated with sugar. As in the Sauternais, the vintage is left until late October, and forays are made through the vines at intervals of ten days or so, in order that the ripest, most perfect fruit can be selected on each occasion. The great vintages occur in years of long, hot summers, when early morning mists are conducive to the development on the grapes of a particular fungus, Botritis Cynerea. This "noble rot", *pourriture noble*, concentrates the minerals and sugars; the grapes become shrivelled raisins containing but a single glorious golden drop of rich sweetness. Fermentation is prolonged, taking a month or more; the resulting wine is a deceptively alcoholic straw gold nectar. An alcohol content of 15° is cloaked by a dulcet, honeyed taste; summer picnics where fresh apricots or peaches have been washed down with copious draughts of this apparently light enchanting wine can lead to profound somnolence. On more than one occasion it is the Quarts de Chaume served at such a generous repast that has been blamed for turning a second act at Glyndebourne into the most expensive siesta in the world.

With the finest Quarts de Chaume or Bonnezeaux of the greatest years, it appears that time can work no change other than for good; the richness is transformed into elegance and complexity, the colour deepens and all virtues are enhanced.

The even more minute *vignoble* of Bonnezeaux lies a little to the south east, where the soil is slatier and the gradients even steeper. For us, Bonnezeaux, particularly old Bonnezeaux, is even more attractive than Quarts de Chaume, to all the superlative qualities of which is added a faint, fascinating aromatic herbiness.

Preliminary research in advance of our first passage through the vineyards of Bonnezeaux revealed that the most renowned proprietor was also the doyen of the wine makers there. Jean Boivin was kind enough to send us his tariff; the prices were so astronomic as to send us into a state of near shock. We somewhat impolitely neglected to reply to M. Boivin's letter, deciding to examine the rest of the field. The obvious second choice was Madame Fourlinnie, of Les Gauliers, a dark, forbidding house near Thouarcé. The identifying topographical feature that marks Les Gauliers is the vestigial wooden skeleton of an old windmill at the nearby crossroads. This is not necessarily as helpful as might at first be thought; there are dozens of such structures in the vicinity.

The widowed Madame Fourlinnie explained to us that it was her brother living nearby who expertly supervised the making of her wine. He was summoned by telephone to meet us; we were embarrassed to find ourselves being introduced to Jean Boivin. Tactfully, he did not refer to our one-sided correspondence; instead, he patiently and lovingly delineated the history of Bonnezeaux and the intricacies of its vinification.

During the last eight years, we and our clients have been remarkably fortunate in having the privilege of sharing the small stock of legendary older vintages in Madame Fourlinnie's cellar. We have received vociferous pleas to export any existing old Bonnezeaux to Australia, at whatever cost. We are resisting all blandishments and have imposed a strict, yet fair, allocation on the thirsty but appreciative Antipodeans.

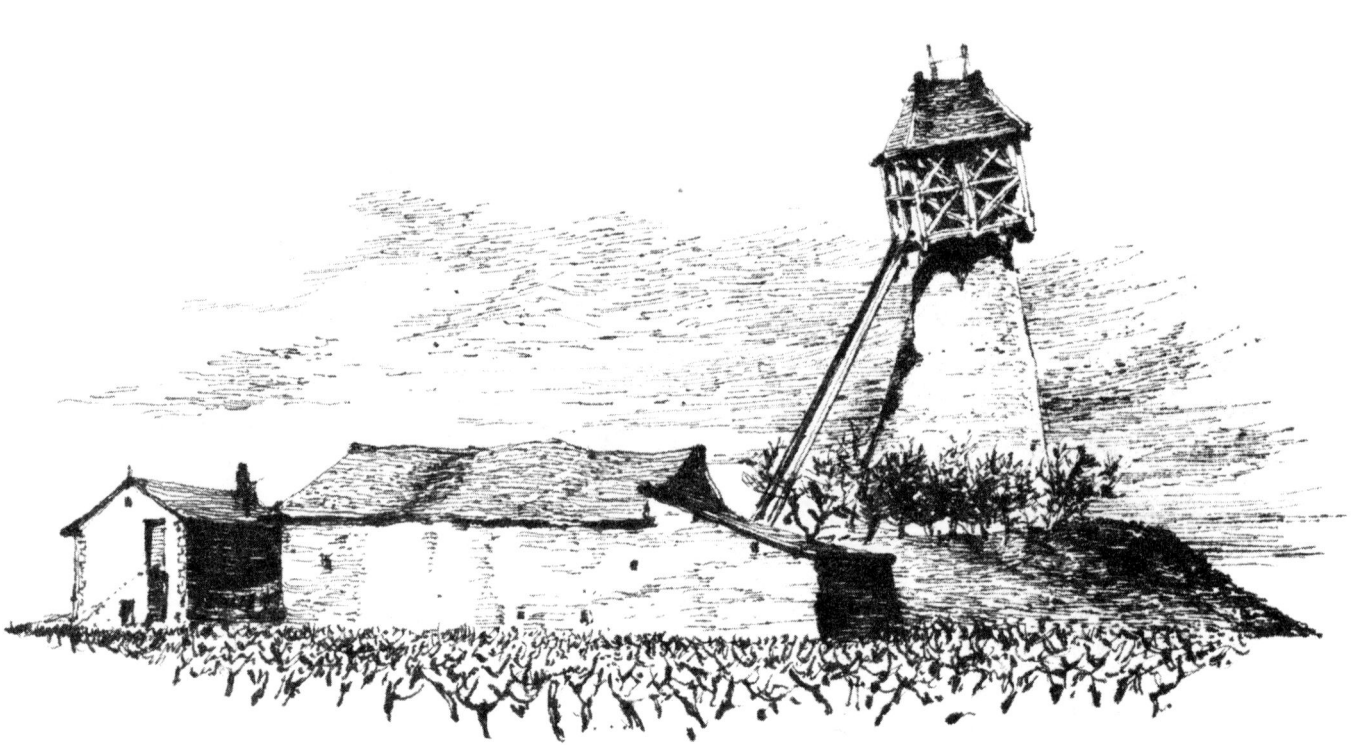

SAUMUR

The château of Saumur stands high above the town and river in magnificent grandeur, although much less ornately towered and crenellated than it appears in an enchanting miniature in a fifteenth century illuminated manuscript, the Duke de Berry's Très Riche Heures. In the foreground of this jewel-like picture, peasants are harvesting grapes. Wine making remains an important part of the town's economy, but the vines have retreated to the hills behind and, east, to the slopes above the Loire, as Saumur has expanded.

Mostly white wine is produced, and the greater part of this is made into an excellent sparkling wine by the *méthode champenoise*. The larger, well-known establishments, *négociants* who buy in grapes from the surrounding countryside, are based at Saint Hilaire-Saint Florent, west of Saumur; their wines are well made, and offer good value. However, our personal preference is for the *mousseux* made by the *Cave Coopérative des Vignerons de Saumur,* formed by a group of small growers in 1948, and now with a membership approaching three hundred.

It would be all too easy to get hopelessly lost in seeking out the *Coopérative's* premises in the hills several kilometres south east of Saumur; small, arrowed signs have been thoughtfully placed at every conceivable bend in the complex maze of lanes around the village of Saint Cyr-en-Bourg, to guide visitors to the small, plain surface buildings. These mark an amazing underground network of tunnels and caves, hidden twenty-five metres below the encircling vines. The main entrance to the cellars lies more than a kilometre away. One drives down a ramp, with headlights on, into a tunnel that twists and turns for a considerable distance before it widens into an enormous cavern.

A tour should not be undertaken lightly; the cellars cover more than eight acres, and the forceful chief *caviste*, M. Marquès, will not be prepared to let you dodge a detailed explanation on any of the operations that he supervises.

At the centre of the labyrinth, vast cement *cuves* lie directly below hoppers, twenty-five metres above, into which the grapes are tipped during the *récolte*; they fall through an *égrappoir*, which removes the stalks and leaves, descend further to the *pressoir*, until the juice flows into the fermentation *cuves*. Many tunnels are lined with high walls made up of thousands of crown capped bottles stacked horizontally; here they rest for the nine months during which secondary fermentation takes place. In the furthest recesses stand rank upon rank of *pupitres*, in the slots of which rest rows of horizontally placed bottles. These must be given a part-turn each day, and over a period of two months be gradually inverted until vertical, when the waste products of the secondary fermentation will rest upon the cap. This apparently simple manoeuvre requires great skill, and it is M. Marquès, a native of Champagne, who undertakes the task, giving an accurate and subtle twist to thirty thousand bottles each day.

Elsewhere in the cellars, removal of the sediment, *dégorgement*, is performed manually. This is a highly dexterous operation whereby pressure within the bottle forces out the sediment, to be replaced by a proportion of wine mixed with cane sugar, calculated to produce the required degree of dryness or sweetness. The bottles are stacked away for a further few months, and are finally released for dispatch when the contents have achieved a balance that completely satisfies M. Marquès and his colleagues.

Although the main commerce of the *vignerons* of Saint Cyr-en-Bourg derives from their justly admired *mousseux*, it is the still wine that wins them most acclaim. Fragrant, pebbly dry and invigoratingly fresh, the Saumur Blanc of Saint Cyr unfailingly collects the Gold Medal at the *Concours Agricole* in Paris each March; its annual success, unbroken for

many years, is probably itself a record. In his concise but highly informative Wines of France, Mr. Cyril Ray points out the similarity between the chalky soil of the rolling hills around Saumur, and that of the *coteaux* of Champagne, opining that to be the reason for the distinct resemblance between the still wines of both regions.

Saumur Champigny, the red wine of the district, merits a great deal more attention than it seems to get. The *cabernet franc*, an important part of the *cépage* of Saint Emilion and Pomerol, makes a softer, fruitier wine in these more northern latitudes. The version of Saint Cyr is fairly light in colour and body; when served at cellar temperature, as is the local custom, it is a refreshing summer beverage.

The village of Chaintres lies in the hills between Saint Cyr-en-Bourg and the Loire. The vineyards are divided into *clos* by limestone walls, the cottages, houses and châteaux, of which there are several, are all constructed from the same beautiful white stone. The large grottoes that serve as local cellars were created by the excavation of these huge blocks of *tuffeau*. Had his engravings been of cellars rather than prisons, those below Paul Filliatreau's small house would have entranced Piranesi. The steep, tortuous pathways, high rough-hewn arches vanishing into shadow, cave leading into cave, vast barrels wedged into place by stout timbers, the scene has a fantastic, almost nightmare quality that Piranesi would have surely relished; and it is also an ideal place for the slow maturation of Paul's fine, red wine. A friendly, well-built man in his mid-thirties, Paul Filliatreau's easy going manner conceals an intense passion regarding the making of wine. He owns *clos* in various parts of the village, and firmly believes in a separate vinification for each of them. In the last few years, Paul has used the abundant harvest from the younger vines to make a charming, fruity Saumur Champigny *primeur* that is quickly sold to the restaurants of the area. The *appellation* authorities have dropped a hint that they are so impressed with the wine that Paul will get an unheard-of special dispensation of an earlier release date than the official December 15th in future years.

A happy concomitant of the quick sale of the *primeur* is that Paul can thereafter devote his energies to the splendid traditional-style wine that he makes by skilfully marrying ancestral methods with all the possibilities to be gained from modern technology. A new building behind the house contains a battery of stainless steel *cuves*; steel tubing that spirals around each of them reveals that the temperature of fermentation can be minutely controlled. Traditionally, the *chapeau*, a dense mass of skins, pips and stalks that rises to the surface of the fermenting juice, should be trodden into the wine several times a day by foot. Other *vignerons* have abandoned the time-consuming method; Paul, working on his own, finds it increasingly difficult to deal with the *chapeau*, but knows that the routine is necessary to give his wine its strong, dark colour and enormous depth of fruity flavour. The first *cuve* is an extraordinary prototype; a close-fitting grid can be made to descend through the wine several times a day, bearing the *chapeau* ahead. The system has as yet to prove its worth, but Paul anxiously hopes that it is the solution to his problem.

Thereafter, the wine rests in barrel underground until the malolactic fermentation has finished, and the esters and essences that go into a fine wine have amalgamated into a perfectly balanced relationship. Unlike most other Saumur Champigny, the Filliatreau wine should be kept until the tannin it contains has softened into a liaison with the fruit; after eight years or ten years it becomes a liquor to remember.

Paul has recently acquired a small *clos* containing gnarled old vines that are more than one hundred years old, pre-dating the scourge of phylloxera in the late nineteenth century. Although their total harvest barely suffices to fill one small barrel, we hope that Paul Filliatreau has heeded our pleas and that a proportion, however small, will eventually find its way to Mere.

CHINON, BOURGUEIL AND
SAINT NICOLAS-DE-BOURGUEIL

The Loire Valley has been described as the 'Garden of France', a tribute to the loveliness and the lushness of its countryside; if so, Touraine may be called the "Kitchen Garden." The soil is rich and fertile, the configuration of the terrain creates a mild microclimate and, just as at Ampuis in the Rhône, the first shoots of asparagus appear in the carefully tilled fields of Touraine, the first petits pois, lettuces, radishes, strawberries, to be harvested and quickly dispatched to the cornucopian markets of the cities. In September and October Touraine presents an aspect of golden abundance; polythene-covered sheds hold row upon row of suspended bundles of bronze-brown tobacco leaves, huge ochre pumpkins are ripe for picking, long tall mesh-covered structures, *séchoirs*, are brimful with the tasselled topaz cobs of freshly harvested maize. The grapes in the vineyards have ripened too, and the vintage is about to start.

Chinon, Bourgueil and Saint Nicolas-de-Bourgueil are considered, with justification, to be the best red wines of the Loire Valley. Even so, they are not immediately ingratiating; perseverance is required before their undoubted charms are revealed to the newcomer. Relatively low in alcohol in comparison with the fat, liquorous wines made in hotter latitudes, yet endowed with a plenitude of tannin, the taste of fruit tends to be obscured by a dry slatiness when the wine is young. There are many who relish the wines at this stage, and the vast bulk is consumed within a year of the vintage. What a loss; careful and patient ageing is essential if the enthusiast is to experience the subtleties that have given these wines their reputation.

The stone houses of Chinon are terraced above the Vienne six kilometres before it joins the Loire; the panorama of the confluence of the two rivers seen from the high ground behind the stoutly fortified church of Candes Saint Martin is perhaps the finest view in the Loire Valley. The château of Chinon dominates the town, and is a reassuring sight for English eyes; with its motte and bailey it bears a far closer resemblance to the medieval castles of Britain than to the other châteaux of the Loire.

The vineyards spread behind the château, and to the villages further up the Vienne. On one side of the road the river bends sinuously through meadows, thick banks of reeds, osiers and groves of tall, slender poplars; on the other hand lie fields of vines and the white stone cottages and houses of the growers. Behind the village of Panzoult, the Desbourdes' establishment is graced by an imposing carved limestone entrance arch; the house itself comes as something of an anti-climax. Caves in the rock behind the yard house farm implements and livestock, dozens of hutches containing plump Belgian rabbits en route to Mme. Desbourdes' kitchen; scraggy turkeys parade the yard, oblivious of their eventual fate.

Raymond Desbourdes is a small, earnest, bespectacled man who cares deeply about his Chinon, though his production is modest. He is prepared to delay his *récolte*, the risk of deterioration in the weather notwithstanding, if he considers that the grapes need extra days in which to gain more sugar and fruit. In his hands the *cabernet franc* is transformed into a dark, well-balanced classic Chinon that will demonstrate a perfect relationship between the various elements when time has effected an equilibrium between them. Twenty-five kilometres northwest of Chinon, Bourgueil and Saint Nicolas-de-Bourgueil are the centres of an equally important red wine area; here too the *cabernet franc* produces the stylish wine for which the region is famed. Bourgueil is a busy market town constructed from the local limestone. The north side of the solidly built church is cluttered with a muddle of abutting shops; the *halles*, market hall, has a colonnade of graceful white stone arches; on the corner, in the bar of the *Grand Hôtel du Commerce,* no matter what time of day, a group of old men will be discussing the vintage prospects or politics over a carafe or two of wine, while the youth of the town attempt to beat the system on noisy, brightly-lit pintables. The butcher next door has hung a *sanglier*, a wild boar, outside; on the wall beside the entrance of the *Hôtel de l'Écu de France* an enamel plaque, unfaded by time, promises that within lie *cabinets de société*, for *noces et banquets*, that a piano is available and that there is a *service de trains*, horse cabs, to meet passengers arriving at the station of nearby Port-Boulet.

Clos de la Contrie is to be found between Bourgueil and Saint Nicolas, separated from the road by its vineyard, and secluded behind walls in a copse of pines. The nineteenth century house is typical of the region. Claude and Hélène Ammeux are extraordinarily hospitable, and insist that we make their home our base when visiting Touraine. Hélène is a superb cook who delights in producing the specialities of the region from her small kitchen, *matelote d'anguilles*, a stew of eels and mushrooms simmered in red wine, pumpkin soup, the pumpkin serving as a bowl, a dark, rich *daube* made from the wild boar already seen in Bourgueil, and so on. Naturally we accept the pressing invitation with alacrity, always bearing in mind that it is essential to be in training beforehand. The need for health and fitness is not only because of the gastronomic assault course provided by Hélène, but also because the Ammeux family keeps Spanish hours. Early evening is occupied by last minute shopping, and a *pastis* or two with friends in the *Commerce;* then Hélène incarcerates herself in the kitchen, spurning all offers of assistance, while Claude conducts us to the *chai* for a comprehensive tasting. Aperitifs do not appear before nine o'clock, and asparagus, fresh from the garden, is not served until ten. The wines that accompany the earlier dishes are of fairly recent vintage, but pass back in time as night advances. In the early hours, with the cheese, Claude with a flourish will produce a dusty bottle that he has been concealing in a cupboard; the limpid ruby contents will be delicately transferred to our glasses and, at last, the high-flown phrases of poetic wine writers begin to make sense. An old bottle such as this, perhaps of the 1959 vintage, is indeed a jewel-like miracle, and one can willingly concur with allusions to the fragrance of violets, raspberries and truffles, or with Rabelais' epithet, that Chinon and Bourgueil slip down the throat "like taffeta."

Most wine drinkers feel that Master Rabelais would have been a good friend; a man who described wine as "the good September soup" must have had a well adjusted sense of proportion, and obviously regarded a few good bottles as an essential concomitant to man's wellbeing. A handsome statue of Rabelais adorns the river bank in Chinon, and his image is borne on bottle labels and cartons, encircled by his resounding motto: *beuvez tousjours, ne mourrez jamais*. Raymond Desbourdes and Claude Ammeux share Rabelais' idea of the joy of life; they employ their skills to make wines worthy of the Master's favour.

[37]

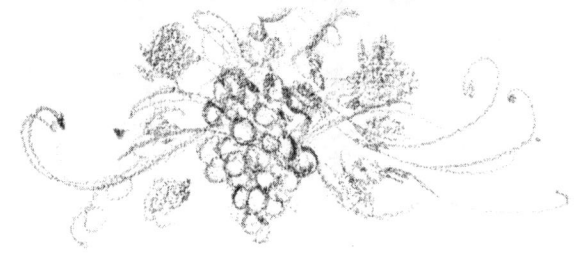

AZAY-LE-RIDEAU

Moated, turreted Azay-le-Rideau is the most fairy tale-like château in all the Valley of the Loire, but the majority of summer visitors never learn of the white wine made in Azay and the surrounding district. Again, the vine is the *chenin blanc*, or *pineau de la Loire*.

The loveliest and most tranquil of the vineyard villages is Saché, seven kilometres from Azay, further up the slowly meandering river Indre. Some rooms in the solidly fortified château of Saché have been painstakingly transformed into an evocative remembrance of the time when Honoré de Balzac was a frequent visitor. He used the countryside around as a setting for a number of novels; an open book on his desk, spectacles laid at its side, gives a strong illusion that Balzac himself might at any moment return from a vigorous walk through the fields.

We paused in our hunt for Gaston Pavy to picnic in a luxuriantly flower-filled meadow by the river. As we lay by the sluggish water, contemplating the dragonflies poised above the water lilies, we little realised that, beyond the sunken punts and drooping willows, the small white cottage that formed a distant focus to the idyllic scene was the object of our expedition. Fortified and rested, we eventually presented ourselves at the cottage door. It was necessary to reassure a somewhat confused M. Pavy, who was convinced that foreigners could only be calling to ask for directions to Azay-le-Rideau. Soon we were walking along a peaceful, shady lane to investigate the Pavy cellar. The motto *Chai de mon Plaisir* is carved above the stout iron doors that secure the tunnels excavated by Gaston's grandfather in 1899.

Most of the wine made here is crisp, and very dry, but in the good years Gaston makes a small amount of a traditional semi-sweet *moelleux*. In disastrous years, like 1977, there is no wine at all; as elsewhere in the Loire, cruel, biting frosts in late April burned away the emergent buds, and with them any prospect of wine. The hard, slogging labour had to be endured for the rest of the year in the full knowledge that it would produce no benefit other than the survival of the vines, to take their chance again next season.

When obtainable, *moelleux* Azay-le-Rideau exhibits the same incredible ability to age with grace and distinction, as other wines made from the *chenin blanc*. The passing of the years sees the pale yellow liquid gradually darken, the flavour augment in sweetness and complexity of character: when forty or fifty years old, such a wine of a good vintage can be the peer of a similarly venerable Bonnezeaux or Vouvray. We have reverently participated in ritualistic tastings of the legendary vintages of 1921 and 1933, to be spellbound by the sheer perfection of these ambrosial amber essences.

Strolling back to the cottage, we paused to examine an ancient *distillerie ambulante*, which was chugging away beside the lane to produce a deceptively innocent-looking but lethally strong *marc*. Gaston enthusiastically dragged us up a steep bank, so that we might admire his *vignoble*. As we scaled the rise, a dense carpet of green-leaved vines was suddenly revealed, the colour changing, lightening and darkening in ripples as breezes brushed the hillside. Two large, ultra-modern buildings crowned the slope, engulfed in the sea of green. When Gaston referred to a famous sculptor, we guessed that we were looking at the studio and house of the renowned American artist, Alexander Calder. Having a mutual friend, and because Gaston knew him well, we made an impromptu decision to call, bearing a bottle of Azay *moelleux* 1947. We picked our way through a throng of immensely tall brightly-coloured steel mobiles, slowly turning and clanking in the wind. Calder and his wife were very welcoming, and a party developed. It was with great difficulty that we resisted their invitation to stay for dinner, but we had to resume our usual rush along the Loire. Thereafter, we paused at Saché each year, to enjoy the Calders'

conversation in their beautiful house, the walls hung with paintings by Miro, Léger and others, all gifts from the artists. Calder, already in his eighties, liked a glass, or a bottle or two, of good wine as much as anyone. A French doctor had gravely pronounced that his ailments required a regular liberal dose of wine, but—typically French—advised that that made on the doorstep was quite unsuitable, as were the red wines of Bourgueil and Chinon from just along the river. The only elixir that would serve the case was a particular, rather expensive Pomerol (owned by the doctor's cousin?). It certainly made a pleasant change for us to share Sandy's medicine after days spent tasting Loire wines. Alas, its efficacy proved all too short-lived: Alexander Calder died in 1977. Our visits to Saché and to Gaston Pavy are tinged with sadness nowadays, as we glance up at the empty house where we spent so many happy hours.

JASNIÈRES

Three kilometres north-east of La Chartre-sur-le-Loir, standing in the quiet main street of the village of Lhomme, it is possible to discern a low line of gently undulating hills to the east. At close range, however, it is at once obvious that the apparent softness of the contour is delusory; in truth, the slopes are steep and face directly south. At this more northern latitude, thirty kilometres north of the Loire Valley, it is precisely the favourable exposure and the steepness that permits the *chenin blanc*, ubiquitous grape of the mid-Loire, to survive and fruit at all. As an additional precaution, the vines are planted on the lower parts of the slopes, thus being afforded more protection from late frosts and the chilly blast of the north wind.

Our first detour to investigate this place and its curious wine, Jasnières, proved a depressing experience. There was an unmistakable aura of decline about the vineyards; many were overgrown with weeds, others totally abandoned. Of the few reputable growers left, none would part with stock, although we were vouchsafed a couple of tantalizing opportunities to taste the wine. Several years later, it was apparent that a sense of revival was in the air. The eleven acres of Les Caves aux Tuffières, at the centre of the *vignoble*, were looking immaculate. A dynamic young grower, Jean-Baptiste Pinon, had made the decision to invest his skill, energy and slender financial resources in the future of Jasnières. Until his advent at Lhomme, Jean-Baptiste had been producing a *rosé*, more grey than pink, on a couple of acres at nearby Montoire. This little-known

V.D.Q.S. wine, called Coteaux Vendomois, is made from the rare *pineau d'Aunis*.

Having succeeded in marketing an esoteric wine like the Vendomois, Jean-Baptiste shrewdly reckoned that with sufficient hard work and with great care in vinification, it ought to be possible to restore Jasnières to something like its former eminence and, at the same time, to survive financially. Behind the massive nineteenth century cast-iron doors of Les Caves aux Tuffières lie labyrinthine cellars, hewn from the limestone below the vineyards. The original excavation was to provide the huge blocks of stone from which the houses of the region are built. Strange vertical grooves in the walls show where wooden wedges were beaten in and soaked with water, to swell and detach the stone. Apart from the firmly locked private library of ancient vintages, the property of the former owner, the widow Langlois, the enormous grottoes were initially void of stock. An eerie, pale miasma on the sandy floor of the furthest, darkest recesses proved to be a crop of endives that the economically-minded Pinons had prudently planted. Happily, Jean-Baptiste has totally justified his self-confidence. Long rows of bottles line the walls, and the Pinon Jasnières finds an eager, ready market. Dry, fine and sinewy when young, the taste belies the rich fruitiness that will eventually arrive with bottle age. Those lucky enough to have experienced wines from the legendary vintages of the 1920's aver that the passage of time produces a miraculous transformation, the wines developing a deep, golden-brown hue and a soft, sweet entrancing flavour.

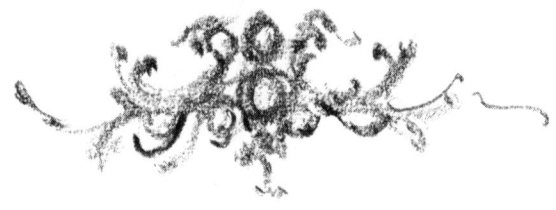

VOUVRAY AND MONTLOUIS

The wines of Vouvray and of Montlouis are very, very similar; so alike that it is extremely difficult to distinguish between them at a "blind" tasting. When obliged, as now, to point any nuances that each may have, we would suggest that Vouvray is more *nerveuse*, compact and muscular, Montlouis rather softer and more rounded. The lack of differentiation is hardly surprising; the same grape, the *chenin blanc*, is grown in similar soil at the identical latitude. In both places the vineyards are canted toward the sun, the slopes offer the same protection, and the vines are cultivated in the self-same way.

Both at Vouvray and Montlouis the still wines range from a fine dry *nature sec* to a mouth-filling, chewy, fruity *demi-sec* to, in the great vintages that only happen several times each century, a fabulously rich, unctuous, golden-brown *moelleux*. Further, the techniques of Champagne are employed at both places to furnish wines that vary from a lightly frothy *pétillant* to a fully sparkling *mousseux*, either of which can be made as anything from a crisp, fresh *brut* to a full, flavoursome *demi-sec*. All tastes are catered for; everyone can find a Vouvray or Montlouis that is grateful to his palate.

The *vignobles* brace the Loire ten kilometres east of Tours, Vouvray north and Montlouis south of the river. The small towns face each other across the water, but the nearest bridges are at Tours and, fifteen kilometres east, at Amboise. This presents an annoying and frustrating inconvenience when, having spent a busy afternoon tasting wine in one place, we are anxious to terminate the day's work in the other as quickly as possible. These wine towns are ideally situated; through the ages, the river has cut through the soft limestone to leave cliff-like banks which are honeycombed with cellars and troglodytic dwellings, some of which have been in use for many centuries. On May 2nd 1644, John Evelyn went for a boat trip on the Loire and duly recorded the experience in his diary. 'Leaving the castle (of Amboise) we passed Mount Louis. This is a village having never a house above ground, but such as are hewn out of the main rock only. Here and there the funnel of a chimney appears through the surface of the vineyards which are over them; and in this manner they inhabit the caves on one side of the river for many miles.'

At Rochecorbon the impressive cellars of Marc Brédif are surmounted by an elegant eighteenth century mansion. That its handsome façade is something of a fake is revealed by a glance at the side walls; they are only three or four feet wide; the rooms of the building have been hewn from the rock behind. The wide, arched entrance to the cellars is flanked by statues of Saint Vincent and John the Baptist, the patron saints of *vignerons* and *cavistes* respectively, as André Chevreau, the relaxed and soft-spoken chief *caviste*, is quick to point out. The tunnels were excavated in Roman times, and stretch far below the vineyards above. At the furthest limit of the cave system iron doors guard a circular, ceremonial tasting room. Niches in the rock contain bottles of vintages long past, a mere handful remaining of the earliest, 1874. The present Director of *Les Établissements* Brédif, Jacques Cartier, is a dignified, cultured man who is fully imbued with a sense of the firm's history; he has no intention of ever allowing a bottle of Vouvray to pass the gates that in any way falls short of the ideals expected by his late father-in-law, and established by former generations of Brédifs early in the last century.

We first met Michel Berger at eight o'clock on a May morning, having noted the location of his cellars, Les Caves des Liards, as we sped through Saint Martin-le-Beau, just south of Montlouis, late the preceding evening. One day of misery, a *crise gastrique*, seems an inevitable part of each buying trip, resulting from the abundance and richness of the good food with which our grower friends insistently ply us twice daily; we end up knowing how it must feel to be a Strasbourg goose. We were feebly recovering from just such a day when we knocked at the Bergers' door. No answer was forthcoming; we crossed the road and entered the cellars. We penetrated bottle-lined tunnels until we discovered a small bar where visitors are regaled with a comprehensive tasting of the Berger wines. Michel was moodily washing glasses left over from some bacchanalian session of the previous evening. An empathy was immediately born between us; Michel recognized our sorry state as easily as we perceived his problem, a *gueule de bois*, a hangover.

Michel and his brother Jean are wiry, energetic men who have, by their industry and skill, won a tremendous local reputation. The wines they make are medal winners; their fame as makers of sparkling wine is such that there is a waiting list of growers from a wide area who want the Berger *Frères* to undertake the *champenisation* of their wines. The lucky ones bring their still wine to the Berger cellars in large enamel *cuves* perched on a tractor-drawn trailer. Jean removes the *cuves* with his *chariot elevateur*, fork-lift truck, and the complicated time consuming process of *méthode champenoise* begins. A year or so later the owner returns to collect his bottles of *mousseux*. Good though these will be, they can never excel the Berger home product, as Jean and Michel own the most favoured slopes in the region.

SANCERRE AND
POUILLY BLANC FUMÉ

Sancerre and Pouilly Blanc Fumé are undoubtedly the most renowned of the dry white wines of the Loire; alas, they are also the most expensive. They command a high price because they are famous, because they are in short supply and because they are superb wines. Forty years ago both were counted among the "little" wines of France and were virtually unknown outside the region. The writer, G. B. Stern, who had an extensive knowledge of the Médoc and of Burgundy, was delighted and astonished when in 1926 she first tasted a wine that was totally new to her, a curiosity called Sancerre. With the spread of motor travel the vineyards became accessible to Parisians, particularly those travelling on the main route to the south, the RN7, which passed through the centre of Pouilly-sur-Loire. Gradually the wines became fashionable; enterprising restaurateurs would travel from Paris once or twice a year to purchase stock from the grower of their choice, until no self-respecting Paris bar could have any pretension to a decent wine list without an example or two of Sancerre or Pouilly Blanc Fumé.

Both *vignobles* have been expanded to the maximum area permitted under *appellation* law. Steep slopes that were formerly considered too difficult to cultivate have been brought into production, in some cases by using the ingenious expedient of a rope-drawn plough, capable of being pulled up even the most precipitous slopes by a petrol motor, a system very much akin to the steam ploughs that were once active in parts of Dorset and Wiltshire. Despite this increase in volume, there is insufficient Sancerre or Pouilly Blanc Fumé to satisfy world demand; under the

Georges Guyot

circumstances, it is honourable of the growers not to have exploited their sellers' market more than they have.

Sancerre is an attractive, historic hill-top town south of the Loire, caught in the bend where the river changes course after its two hundred kilometre journey north from the mountains of the *Massif Central*, to flow powerfully and steadily west, eventually joining the Atlantic Ocean near the city of Nantes. Pouilly-sur-Loire lies ten kilometres east, on the further bank of the river. At both places the *sauvignon* is grown; in the Médoc a component in the rich, unctuous dessert wines of the Sauternais, here the soil type and method of vinification produce a startlingly different sort of wine. Crisp and characterful, with a fragrance that conjures up spring hedgerows and a tangy taste reminiscent of black-currants, Sancerre and Pouilly Blanc Fumé have earned their reputation. Pouilly Blanc Fumé seems to gain with some bottle age, and is at peak a year or more following the vintage, whereas Sancerre gives maximum pleasure within a year of bottling; both will remain extremely potable for four or five years.

The Guyots, father and son, live on opposite sides of the main street, the only street, of the sleepy village of Les Loges, on the north bank of the Loire, three kilometres west of Pouilly. We knocked on the son's door one cold January day ten years ago; Christine, Jean-Claude's pretty wife, gave us directions how to find the others among the vines on steep slopes

[47]

above the river. Jean-Claude and his parents were finishing the *taillage*, the pruning of unwanted growth from the previous season. Mme. Guyot was burning the prunings in a mobile incinerator, a wheelbarrow fashioned from an oil drum.

Georges strolled over to greet us, faintly amused that the fame of the family's wine should have been discovered by English wine merchants. While explaining that there was no wine to spare for new customers, he took an entire camembert from the trouser pocket of his blue overalls and unconcernedly proceeded to devour the lot with the aid of a formidable pocket-knife. However, the three of them were only too happy to take half an hour from their back-breaking work in the keen wind in order to show us the excellence of their wine.

It was frustrating in the extreme to be vouchsafed a glimpse of the outstanding quality of the Guyots' luscious wine, knowing that we were unable to purchase a single bottle. Evidently our full hearted appreciation in the minute, barrel-lined cellar gained us some sympathy; after a whispered family conference, Georges turned to suggest that we should call again at about the same time the following year, when they hoped to be able to furnish us with a few, perhaps twenty, cases. Luckily for us and for our customers, in the succeeding years we have gradually weaned away more and more of the Guyots' wine; we try not to think too much about what has befallen the locals who used to buy it all.

With Jean Vatan the first problem was to find his house, a cottage in a jumble of others in the hamlet of Chaudoux, hidden in the rolling hills four kilometres due west of Sancerre. Once found, Jean required a deal of reassurance. Having not travelled further than one hundred kilometres from Chaudoux in his life, meeting strange English people was almost as alarming an encounter as would have been the sudden apparition of Martians. Communication was far from simple, as Jean's French was not a great deal better than our own. After fifteen minutes of patient explanation that our intentions were of the friendliest nature, Jean relaxed sufficiently to lead the way down into his tiny cellar. Having drawn a pipette-full of wine from one of the half dozen barrels standing against the whitewashed wall, he filled our tumblers to the brim and

Jean Vatau

[49]

watched with attentive curiosity as we assayed the liquid. That first taste is utterly unforgettable; it was without doubt the finest example of Sancerre that we had ever encountered. Our incredulous reaction, our unconcealable glee and delight were instantly registered by the short, stout *vigneron*, although it caused him no surprise: Jean Vatan knows full well that he makes a special wine. Conversation was immediately easier, our credentials as appreciative people established, and we were set to become friends.

In the ten years that have passed, our French has improved considerably—there was plenty of room for that—as has Jean's; his probably because the ten children have come back from school with a more acceptable version. He still addresses the pickers in *patois* during the harvest, and is liable to slip into dialect when excited; the wine has not changed—there was no margin for improvement there. In 1972 we arrived by chance on the first day of the vintage, and spent a half day picking *pinot noir* grapes. Romantic as is the notion of helping with the harvest, several hours are quite sufficiently tiring to give the general idea. Before tackling a simple lunch prepared by Jean's wife, Cecile, the *vendangeurs* crushed the black grapes in the wooden tubs in which they had been carried back from the fields, by pounding the fruit with stout wooden cudgels.

The macerated grapes would be left like that overnight, sufficient time for the skins to give a delicate pinkness to the juice, before pressing and fermentation. Our comprehension of Jean's French was still fairly minimal; the distinctive crispness and finesse of the Vatan Pinot *rosé* convinced us that Jean had stated that the wine contained 50% *sauvignon*. In truth, it is pure *pinot*; it is the underlying soil, kimmeridge clay, that imparts the characteristic fruity bite that we had always associated with *sauvignon* wines. The knowledge gives us particular pleasure, as our premises in Mere rest on an outcrop of kimmeridge clay that emerges from beneath the Wiltshire Downs. The stratum runs deep below Dorset, reappears at Kimmeridge Bay on the Dorset coast, and resurfaces again at Sancerre, Pouilly-sur-Loire, Chablis and the smaller *vignobles* of Menetou Salon, Quincy and Reuilly.

QUINCY, REUILLY AND
MENETOU SALON

The other places where the *sauvignon* is grown on kimmeridge clay with conspicuous success are Quincy, Reuilly and Menetou Salon. Quincy is a small town eight kilometres south-west of Mehun-sur-Yièvre, itself twenty kilometres west of the lovely city of Bourges, once the capital of the former Dukedom of Berry; the richly coloured stained glass of the ancient cathedral rivals that of Chartres.

Quincy was the second *vignoble* in France to be accorded *appellation d'origine*, second only to Châteauneuf-du-Pape. No satisfactory explanation seems to be forthcoming as to why each bottle label bears the proud slogan *Vin Noble*; presumably it helps to sell the wine, which is often described as having a "steely" quality, though what is meant by that eludes us completely. As made by rugged, weatherbeaten Raymond Pipet, it is a typically dry, supple *sauvignon* wine with the singular fragrance imparted by that vine. Raymond is a relaxed, good-natured man who retains an air of calm even when, as in 1977 and 1978, the vintages have been a disaster. Late frosts in the earlier year, pounding rain during the *floraison*, flowering, and a prolonged hail storm in July 1978, had resulted in two harvests which put together added up to less than half the crop expected in a decent year. Despite the preponderance of empty barrels in his cellar, Raymond is quite unable to control his enthusiasm when he starts to abstract samples from the few that are full; the extraordinary quality of the small amount of wine that he has managed to salvage from the freaks of nature will, he is confident, impress us. He responds to our blandishments for a share, however small, in the meagre resources of his neat *cave* with a grin and a shrug; we realise that Raymond has already mentally apportioned us whatever he can spare.

Adventures with the Pipet family include jolly celebrations and gargantuan meals with Raymond's fraternity of *chasseurs* in small *auberges* hidden away in the Forest of Sologne; the rousing hunting songs are invariably led by the high, quavering voice of Raymond's eighty year old father. There is only one difficulty regarding our visits to the region: that is how to divide our limited time between these kind friends and the equally hospitable Cordier family at nearby Reuilly.

Reuilly is a six minute Pipet-style drive away from Quincy, fifteen kilometres south-west through the fields and woods of this corner of Berry. The Cordiers live at La Ferté, a perplexing conglomeration of cottages and barns on the road to Issoudun. Even after ten years we have difficulty in selecting the right lane and can easily recall the time spent searching out the Cordier house on our first visit.

In the sensible, practical style of French country cottages, the kitchen is the largest and most comfortable room, rightly so as it is here that the family's life is mainly passed. It was into the kitchen that we were first welcomed by Robert; his wife, Aimé, was not too fully occupied with her pots and pans to greet us kindly, although with evident curiosity as to what had brought us. Son Gérard came in from the vines, and was equally charming, as was his wife, Isabelle. They gladly let us taste their wines, and were pleased and amused by our enthusiastic response. We had a bad moment when we learned that there was no stock whatsoever for newcomers; that gloom was somewhat assuaged by an invitation to share the family lunch. Rapport was quickly established, and grew as we took it in turns to cross the farmyard to draw a further jug of wine from the barrels in the cramped cellar beneath the barn; the long repast concluded with assurances from the Cordiers that there would be a small amount of wine waiting for us the following year.

More than half the Cordier wine now comes to Britain; Robert is perhaps the most esteemed of all the growers, and has been President of the *Syndicat Viticole* of Reuilly for the past twenty years; his wine is eagerly sought after, so again we must shoulder the blame for diverting

Raymond Pipet

towards these shores bottles in such clamorous demand in Reuilly and district.

At Easter the town square is the scene of Reuilly's annual *Foire aux Vins*. Each grower takes a small canvas-covered booth from which to vend his wares; *vignerons* come from other areas to promote their wines. In one corner a farmer sells goat cheeses, *crottins*, and finds a ready market; a more grandiose stall in the centre of the square purveys oysters from Chaillevette, on the Atlantic coast. When the *Deputé* has cut a tricolour ribbon stretched across the ceremonial gateway, and after the *Marseillaise* has been played over the public address system, the dignitaries pass from stall to stall, accepting a complimentary glass of wine at each, closely followed by the hoi polloi, who have to pay for their samples. During the past week a brightly coloured wooden building has been erected beside the church and priory; an eye shattering discordance of purple and yellow, pink and blue, it is a mobile dance hall with a name of its own, *Le Printanier*. For the next few evenings it will be the venue for long hours of dancing, nothing *folklorique* these days (the deafening, pulsating sound is now called BOOM!), but today *Le Printanier* is the setting for the official luncheon. Two hundred people, stuffed into uncomfortably tight suits for the occasion, sit down to a long and serious banquet. A dozen oysters come first, with the compliments of the oyster growers of Chaillevette, an assortment of *charcuterie* next, followed by roast guinea-fowl *en croute*, then a generous slice of pink charollais beef with an array of *primeurs*, early spring vegetables; a daunting variety of cheeses is succeeded by a Grand Marnier soufflé, the whole being washed down by an abundance of wine provided by the growers. At five o'clock the diners are persuaded to take a stroll, perhaps to tour the booths again, while the hall is rearranged for the annual celebration of the *vignoble's confrerie*, the *Échansonerie de Reuilly*. The town turns out in force, and by six o'clock the rows of seats are packed; the Grand Council enters in procession, garbed in medieval robes. Homage is paid to the vines grown in the *commune*; the proceedings are punctuated by unison cries of "Sauvignon! Pinot! Gamay!" The finale is the enrolment into the *confrerie* of four or five local personalities; an essential demonstration of the postulant's suitability for membership is supposed to be his ability to decant a full bottle of wine into an enormous goblet and to swallow the contents without pause. The French are a nation obsessed by the condition of their livers; all too often the bottle-drinking facet of the ceremony has to be glossed over, to the patent dissatisfaction of the townsfolk.

Two years ago we were highly honoured to be the first strangers ever asked to join the *Échansonerie*; we showed our gratitude to Robert Cordier by consuming the entire glass in a single draught. This formidable effort was rewarded by an ovation; the English are now looked upon with something akin to admiration, and the loss to the region of Robert's fine wine is considered justifiable.

The 'yard of Reuilly' feat was rendered the easier because the beverage in question was the Cordier white wine. We first went to La Ferté in pursuit of Robert and Gérard's white Reuilly; distinguished and delectable as this wine is, of whatever vintage, a bonus was to discover that the Cordiers also make a robust, fruity red from the *gamay*, and, most marvellous, a fine, pale, delicate *rosé* from the rare *pinot gris*, a wine so prized and in such short supply that it commands a higher price than the white. Ten years ago, Reuilly was virtually unknown in this country, yet now we can sell all that Robert can spare, and the esoteric Pinot Gris can be found in a surprising number of first-class restaurants; it seems a happy outcome to our initial clumsy searchings.

Menetou Salon is a village ten kilometres west of the road from Bourges to Sancerre. Again the combination of kimmeridge clay and the *sauvignon* vine produces a characterful, vibrant white wine, and the *pinot noir* a classic, long-term red. On our first visit the *vignoble* had a sad air of neglect. Among the ill cultivated or totally abandoned vineyards were several that clearly showed their owners' care. One such grower, Jean Teiller, has been our supplier of Menetou Salon, red and white, ever since.

We admire Jean's wines a great deal, but he definitely constitutes one of the hazards of our buying trips. Circumstances (a night or two in Reuilly or Quincy) always conspire to bring us to the Teiller *cave* in the early morning. After a ritualistic tasting of the season's wines, when we have decided which *cuves* have impressed us most, Jean insists on a conference around his kitchen table. A large bottle of *Eau de Vie de Poire William* is produced, *fabrication de la maison*; this fiery liquor has to have been distilled nefariously; no government agency would countenance the existence of such a "fire water." The ordeal by *poire william* is the accompaniment to Jean Teiller's annual treat, which we cannot be so mean as to deny him. Sham though it is, at least an hour of haggling is essential for Jean's sense of decency and contentment. We arrive with an accurate notion of what the wine should cost, given our confidence in the standard of the Teiller wine and our prior knowledge of prices in the rest of the Loire Valley; yet year after year we have to retain our composure and solemnly pretend to argue with Jean until his impossibly optimistic first suggested tariff has been reduced to reality, the price that we had always intended to pay, as we suspect he realises before the meeting is convened.

Happily, the reputation of the wines of Menetou Salon has grown in recent years; they have regained a lot of the fame enjoyed in former times. Today the southern facing slopes present an appearance of prosperity; they are in an immaculate state of cultivation. Our intention, as with the other relatively little-known *sauvignon* wines, is to ensure that sufficient finds its way to Britain, where we hope that a discerning and appreciative public will share our enthusiasm.

SAINT POURÇAIN-SUR-SIOULE

To include the wines of Saint Pourçain-sur-Sioule among those of the Loire is something of a cheat, as the town is one hundred and fifty kilometres south of the nearest fully accredited Loire vineyard, being far nearer the mountains of the Auvergne. However, the rivers Sioule and Allier are undeniably tributaries of the Loire, entering it near La Charité-sur-Loire, and the wines are extremely attractive, so let the classification stand.

Saint Pourçain marks the virtual centre of France, and stands on an important intersection of main routes from the north-east to Spain, from the north-west to Lyon and the south, and from Switzerland to the west coast. A large proportion of the wine that emanates from Saint Pourçain is consumed in the hotels, bars and restaurants of the attractive spa resort of nearby Vichy. Each day hundreds of frail invalids walk slowly and haltingly beneath the white painted canopies of the pathways of the *Parc des Sources*. They are on their way to the gay green and white pavilions where the hot mineral-impregnated waters bubble from the ground; each person clutches a tiny wicker basket in which nestles an official measured Vichy glass. As they leave the bustling, humid pumprooms an hour or so later, their eyes seem brighter and the uncertainty has gone from their gait. Have the restorative waters worked their cure so soon, or is it the anticipation of a good bottle of Saint Pourçain with which to wash down a five course luncheon that has wrought the change?

Saint Pourçain is an ancient town, at one time fortified by an encircling wall. Old houses abound in the narrow back streets, the church of Sainte

Croix is an interesting and peaceful haven in which to pass a reflective and calming half hour after the pressure of an hour or so spent battling through the ceaseless traffic on the busy RN 7 or RN 9. A different sort of oasis is offered by the comfortable *Hotel du Chêne Vert*. Michelin one-star restaurants are just about our ideal, offering good food served pleasantly, with none of the ceremony and ultra-smartness that seems to be obligatory in the two or three-star establishments—although of course we shall bravely continue our selfless investigations into all three types of hostelry. The *Chêne Vert* seems to be more welcoming at each visit; it is just the relaxed sort of place in which to drink the wine of Saint Pourçain on its home ground for the first time, even better if it accompanies Jean Giraudon's *poulet au fromage* or *parfait d'écrevisse*.

The wines, red, *rosé* and white, have V.D.Q.S. status, but in his Wines of France Mr. Cyril Ray tips the white wine as a strong contender for elevation to *appellation d'origine*. Bureaucracy is almost an art form in France, so it may be a long time and a great deal of paperwork before Mr. Ray's prognostication comes to pass. Wine has been made around the town for many centuries, as evidenced by carvings in Sainte Croix, but hardly as a commercial proposition. Each farmer cultivated a few rows of vines to furnish wine for domestic consumption, with little if any to spare for the market place. Control of vinification was haphazard, so the quality of the wine was highly variable.

The *Cave Coopérative* was founded in 1952, as a result of the dynamism and vision of one man, Marcel Edier. It was his enthusiasm and persuasiveness that brought about the grouping together of the small growers, a formidable task in a rural area where accord is the exception and feuding controversy the norm. M. Edier's percipience and confidence were quickly justified; the wines of Saint Pourçain are now widely known and respected; those made at the well-equipped and impeccably organized *Cave Coopérative* are of a high, consistent quality that regularly leads to the receipt of medals at wine competitions held in Paris and elsewhere. Marcel Edier died suddenly in 1976 whilst selling wine from the *Cave's* stand at the *Concours Agricole* in Paris. His successor as Director is François Champfeuil, a charming and friendly young man

whose evident expertise and deep concern for the product has won over even the most cynical among the older growers.

Vine varieties grown at Saint Pourçain are particularly interesting. The pale pink muscular *rosé* and the richer, fruitier red are made from the *gamay Beaujolais* with a very small proportion of *pinot*. Both are pleasant, unpretentious wines that are worth examination, but our particular favourite is the dry white wine. Its *cépage* consists of 50% *tresallier*, a rare vine that is now unique to Saint Pourçain, with varying proportions of *sauvignon*, *pinot chardonnay* and *aligoté*. The wine that results from this blend is deliciously clean and fragrant and, we think, offers remarkable value.

THE RIVER RHÔNE

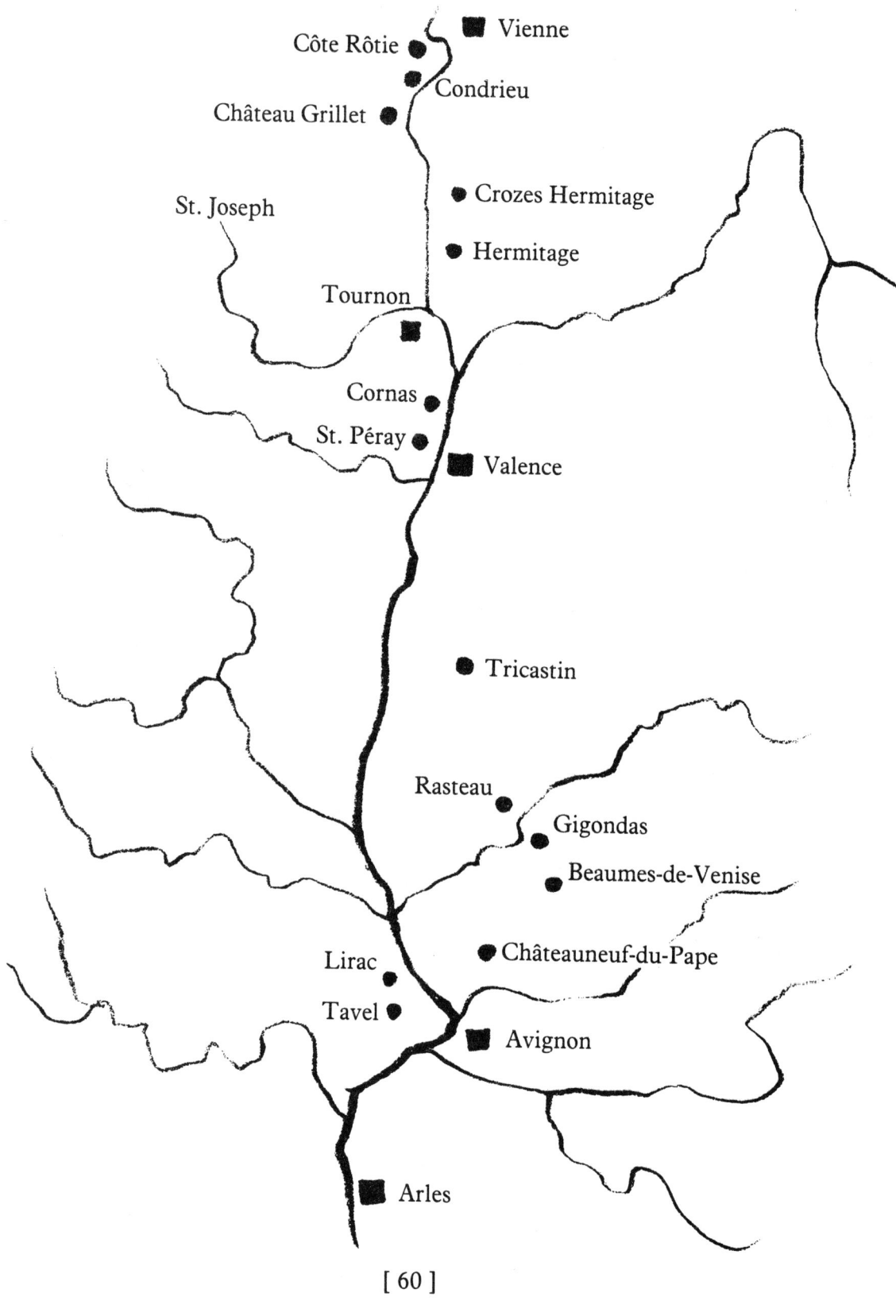

Côte Rôtie

Vienne

Condrieu

Château Grillet

Crozes Hermitage

St. Joseph

Hermitage

Tournon

Cornas

St. Péray

Valence

Tricastin

Rasteau

Gigondas

Beaumes-de-Venise

Lirac

Châteauneuf-du-Pape

Tavel

Avignon

Arles

RHÔNE

CÔTE RÔTIE

The vineyards of the Northern Rhône commence at Ampuis, eight kilometres south of Vienne, thirty-six kilometres south of Lyons, and run south beside the river for sixty kilometres, as far as Saint Péray and Valence.

Vienne is a fascinating town, with narrow streets, old houses, market places, and a multitude of Roman monuments. The Temple of Augustus and Livia, a diminutive version of the *Maison Carrée* in Nimes, is in fine condition, the theatre is virtually complete, the Lapidary Museum is bursting with mosaics and statuary and of course there is the splendid obelisk that served as a marker post for the charioteers in the Hippodrome. The *Pyramide* stands in magnificent isolation, sixty yards from the renowned restaurant which has adopted the same name. The founder of La Pyramide, Fernand Point, exerted an enormous influence on the course of classical French cuisine. He died twenty-five years ago, but neither the standards nor the menu have altered discernibly in the interim. Madame Point, a venerable figure, still scrutinizes all that passes Chez Point. It will be a sad day when she no longer greets her guests.

Ampuis, on the west bank of the river, is one of the most important wine villages of the Rhône. Vines have been grown here since the area was colonized by the Greeks.

The classic vine of the Northern Rhône, the *syrah*, is grown at Tain l'Hermitage and at Ampuis, to produce the two finest and most distinguished red wines of the region. Both Hermitage and Côte Rôtie, the wine of Ampuis, can take as long as fifteen to twenty years to reach maturity, but Côte Rôtie comes to perfection rather the earlier. This is because another grape, the curious white *viognier,* is added to the *syrah.* The *viognier,* a vine that is extremely difficult to grow and sparse in fruit, is found only here and at Condrieu.

The vineyards themselves are well-nigh incredible, consisting of abrupt, stepped terraces retained by drystone walls. Grown on what amounts to more of a cliff than a hillside, the vines can often be only one or two rows deep. Each one is supported on a framework of four stout chestnut poles. It is obvious that vineyard chores must be carried out by hand, there being no possibility of using mechanical implements on such terrain. The effort required simply to mount the terraces is considerable, and the work is back-breaking. Summer heat is so intense that the *vignerons* start at four o'clock and quit the vineyard at eleven o'clock, before conditions become intolerable. However, it is precisely the precipitous nature of the place that creates the splendour of the wine. The hillside faces south-south-east, and each vine receives the full benefit of the sun from daybreak to sunset. Thus, the grapes ripen to perfection.

Each January a small wine fair takes place in the *Salon de Fêtes* in Ampuis on the Monday following the weekend of the big Orange Wine Fair. The *vignerons* set up trestle tables on which to display their wares. In one corner stands a table laden with numbered bottles. Here sit the leading tasters of the district, assaying and assessing samples of Côte Rôtie of the previous vintage. A mere fifteen or so growers make and bottle their own Côte Rôtie. Of these, two names alternate in winning the honours, Jasmin and Champet.

Émile Champet lives by the Rhône, at Le Port, once a thriving quayside. A small, wiry man, with tanned, lined features, his life is divided between a smallholding on the banks of the river and three acres of vineyard on the hill. A favourable microclimate gives vegetation a head start at Ampuis. The early vegetables, or *primeurs,* are famous in France, and the Champets stand market in Vienne, Lyons and elsewhere to sell their spring produce. Their small stock of wine is usually sold by early summer, mainly to people who have heard of its reputation and manage to search out the not-easily located house. Émile prunes his vines severely, thus diminishing the yield but improving the quality. His Côte Rôtie is superb, typical of the wine at its best, but it needs bottle age. The new wine is so tannin-filled as to be almost painful. Like other growers, Émile's gastric tract must be zinc-lined; he swallows his glassful with enormous gusto. Over the years, patient explanation has brought him to the realisation that we are more delicate, and that we must spit out if we are to survive our trip.

The first vintage that we tasted of the Jasmin wine was the 1969, our choice from the wine list of La Pyramide. Very special, this Côte Rôtie was rather different, more subtle, than others. We investigated why this should be next day. Robert Jasmin, a large, amiable man, lives near the market place. His wine, La Chevalière d'Ampuis, is made predominantly from the grapes of old vines. Grandfather Jasmin came from Champagne to be chef at the château of Ampuis. He became enamoured of the principal product of the village, and eventually took over the vineyard of the château. The age of the vines and the fact that Robert uses as much as 12% of the rare *viognier* serve to give his wine its particular character. Unlike other growers, he does not buy yeast. Eight days before the vintage, he picks a hundred kilogrammes of the ripest grapes, and starts a fermentation from the yeasts in the bloom on the skins. This nucleus is then used to start the main fermentation.

As with Champet, our main problem was to persuade Robert to part with his precious product. At the first meeting, we made friends, but no wine was forthcoming. The following year, we received a few token cases. Nowadays we rejoice when we descend to his cellar. Neatly arranged in rows are the fifteen or so *pièces* that represent Robert's total annual harvest. Each *pièce* holds the equivalent of a mere nine hundred bottles. There along one wall stand ranged six of the small barrels, two marked MME. POINT, the other four carrying the heart-warming slogan, YAPP.

Again like Champet's wine, Robert's is tough and uncompromising in youth, with a dark, Tyrian purple hue, and a fearsome amount of tannin. After ten years in bottle, as it reaches or approaches maturity, the flavour and aroma of a classic Côte Rôtie stand revealed; the colour a beautiful, deep vermilion, shot with glints of ruby. Stories of a fabulous bouquet underpinned with hints of violets, raspberries, even truffles, become believable. The taste sets the seal on a wine that would concede nothing to first growth clarets in a comparative tasting, being very complex and deeply satisfying.

CONDRIEU

On the whole, we hope that we manage to eschew the use of wild superlatives, although our customers and friends might not agree. Condrieu is different; here any amount of purple prose is permitted, and we feel at liberty to indulge our affection and reverence for the wine. In fact, Condrieu is our favourite dry, white wine, bar none. A delicate, pale-yellow hue is matched with a unique and magical fragrance that combines muskiness with the perfume of mayblossom; and the flavour, ah, the flavour . . . to say that Condrieu has a vernal freshness reminiscent of springtime conveys our feelings, but does not quite touch the spot. Truthfully, we do not know the adjectives with which to sum up the taste, but we know that it is glorious.

The village of Condrieu lies five kilometres downstream from Ampuis. As there, the vineyards consist of vertiginous terraces carved from the hillside, with ideal exposure towards the south-east. At Ampuis the *vignoble* is obviously prospering, and, where possible, even expanding. At Château du Rozay Paul Multier will indicate the steep slopes below, and explain that what are now impenetrable thickets of brambles, thorns and trees were once immaculately-kept vineyard. Photographs taken in the 1880's show the neat terraces, with numerous workers tending the vines. Once abandoned, nature quickly reclaimed this territory as her own. Paul Multier is a shrewd, intelligent man, who knows a great deal about the region, in particular its viticultural history. He explains that the land was relinquished reluctantly. The *viognier* is an ancient *cépage*, peculiar to Condrieu and to Ampuis. Over the centuries it has become less

Caviste at Rozay

productive, increasingly difficult to grow, and reluctant to bear fruit. It requires much more attention than other vine types, and this care is rewarded by a miserably low yield. Furthermore, manual labour, essential on these precipitous slopes, is difficult to find, and becoming increasingly expensive. Those prepared to endure the fatigue of working such terrain under all weather conditions become fewer and fewer, and the old skills are disappearing. The net result is that very little Condrieu

is made, and the majority of that is consigned to the famous restaurants of the area, *La Pyramide, Bocuse* in Lyons, *Chez René* at Saint Romain-en-Gal, the *Bellevue* over the river at Les Roches-de-Condrieu, the *Beau Rivage* in Condrieu itself, and others, which does not leave many bottles for the world at large. When Paul Multier can show us his entire production of 1978 in the form of two *pièces*, less than two thousand bottles, we thankfully take the twenty cases that he offers, and we certainly do not quibble about the price.

[69]

CHÂTEAU GRILLET

The wine of Château Grillet is even more of a rarity than Condrieu, and even more difficult to lay one's hands on. The tiny vineyard lies in a natural basin which affords nigh-perfect protection against the vagaries of bad weather. This allows the problematic *viognier* to give of its best. The charming small château occupies the centre of the amphitheatre of terraces and vines. The cellars of the château are ridiculously small, but then there is so little wine to store within them. The reputation of Château Grillet has been of the highest for centuries. During that time it has drawn many famous visitors, such as Thomas Jefferson, whilst he was ambassador to France, and Pascal (he of *Pensées* fame, not the *vinificateur* from Vacqueyras). That celebrated gourmet-writer, the self-styled Prince Curnonsky, rated Grillet after Montrachet and Yquem, ahead of Coulée de Serrant and Château Chalon, as the third finest white wine of France. At the inception of the system of *appellation*, when the rights for that distinction were being sparingly distributed, Château Grillet brought off a most remarkable coup. It managed to acquire an *appellation* entirely of its own, the smallest *vignoble* in France to do so.

Kept in barrel for a whole year longer than its neighbour, Grillet becomes somewhat darker than Condrieu and gains an intensity in flavour that indicates its potential longevity. It is only to be expected that a nonpareil in such short supply—not many more than five thousand bottles in 1978—should have become a collector's item.

GAMAY, SYRAH AND
SAINT JOSEPH

The *Cave Coopérative* of Saint Désirat-Champagne stands quite near the RN86. The general effect is that of a rural scene in some Russian film. The large, somewhat seedy-looking mass of the *Cave* is an unlovely, purely functional concrete shell in the design of which no concession to visual pleasure has been made. On one side, a railway line and a platform-less halt are flanked by the tall wooden buildings of a timber yard. Over the road, there is a tiny, neat, vine-clad house, with a pair of heavily pollarded plane trees beside the door. A small sign and a *pétanque* court (a strip of sand) reveal that it is a bar, a veritable *estaminet*, where vineyard workers can pause for refreshment on their way home from the fields.

Although the *cave* is visible from the main road, we had always hurtled past, en route to Tournon and Tain l'Hermitage, usually behind schedule, having spent longer than intended at Condrieu. Early in 1977 we had good reason to call. The whisper had reached our ears that an unusual *cépage* was being grown here, in our territory, and with great success. Preferring in the first instance to preserve our incognito, we merely bought a number of bottles for later sampling, and asked a few questions about the method of cultivation.

Buying the ingredients for a simple picnic from the *charcuterie*, *boulangerie* and *épicerie* of some small town is one of the delights of a springtime journey through France. Nowadays the hospitality of grower friends prevents us from indulging in such treats more than once or twice each trip. Several days had elapsed since our call at Saint Désirat before

we had an opportunity to buy bread, cheese and *jambon cru*. We sat on a hillside which had a panorama over the gorges of the river Ardèche, our nostrils assailed by the pungent scent of wild thyme. Only then did we taste the new wine, a Gamay made from exactly the same grape as Beaujolais. Deliciously fruity and eminently quaffable, it was certainly as good as a well-made Beaujolais, but very much less expensive. We realised at once that we had made an important and valuable find. A truck collected our first consignment just as soon as the *Cave Coopérative* could get the cartons ready. The reaction of our customers has been as enthusiastic as our own; the Gamay of Saint Désirat has proved to be one of our most popular wines.

A year and half a dozen consignments later, we finally met M. Chaleat, the genial director of the *Cave*, and his assistant, M. Cheynel. They explained that viticulture in the area had dramatically declined when so few men returned after the first World War. The cultivated terraces had to be abandoned, and quickly became overgrown. What wine there was supplied home use only—a rough *Vin de Table*. It was M. Chaleat, a fruit farmer, who had the vision and enthusiasm to persuade his neighbours to form a *coopérative* in order to recommence the making of a decent wine. The *appellation* of Saint Joseph applies to all the better vineyards on the west bank of the Rhone, in an area stretching forty kilometres from Mauves, near Tournon, north nearly to Condrieu. The permitted vine is the indigenous *syrah*. Accordingly, the members of the *Coopérative* replanted their land with *syrah*, and soon were making an award-winning Saint Joseph. Later, it occurred to M. Chaleat that the fruit from vines of less than five years old could be made into a worthwhile *Vin de Pays*. Until five years old, the grapes were not classified for Saint Joseph, and had been sold cheaply to a distillery. Simply called Syrah, the wine is extremely palatable, with a spicy, almost peppery taste that is most refreshing. M. Chaleat then had another brainwave, the Gamay. By experimenting with carefully selected clones of *gamay*, the *Cave* succeeded in making the highly enjoyable wine that took us to Saint Désirat in the first place. The growers there can be well satisfied with their excellent triumvirate of very potable wines.

Jean-Louis Grippat is the fifth generation of his family to make fine wine, both red and white, at Tournon. Before that, the Grippats were *vignerons* at Mauves, before that at Saint Péray, so he should know what he is about. Jean-Louis has land in several parts of the *commune*, including a well-exposed piece on the hillside above and behind the Chapoutier vineyard that was the first to receive Saint Joseph *appellation* in 1956. He also has the care of the vines of the *Hospice de Tournon*, high above the town, where there is a spectacular view across the Rhône to the steep slopes of Hermitage. Reflectively tasting one of his *cuves* of red Saint Joseph, Jean-Louis points out that, although it contains a fair amount of tannin, well balanced with fruit, it should not be compared directly with Hermitage. The wine will reach its apogee after four or five years in bottle, perhaps seven or eight for the better years. He reckons that his Saint Joseph makes the more agreeable wine for summer drinking, whilst Hermitage comes into its own as autumn mists roll down the river. Even at this stage, Jean-Louis' young wine carries hints of blackcurrants and raspberries, but will do so much more with the passage of time. The white Saint Joseph, made from the *marsanne*, is a delightful bright, muscular wine. It is something of a surprise to learn that Jean-Louis finds its vinification more complicated and prolonged than that of the red.

HERMITAGE

Coming south on the RN86, one rounds a bend and ahead looms the huge, unmistakable saddle-shape of the great granite mass of the hill of Hermitage, a sight that always gives a lift to our hearts. From this side, Hermitage is cliff-like, craggy and somewhat forbidding. As one passes Saint Jean-de-Muzol its aspect changes dramatically as the full south-western face of Hermitage stands revealed; it is magnificent. High on the northern summit, the tiny, ancient Chapel of Saint Christopher is just discernible. The supposed abode of the perhaps-legendary Crusader recluse, the hermit who gave the hill its name, the Chapel is now classified as an historic monument. It marks part of the Jaboulet vineyard, and is proudly emblazoned on their label. Dotted over the slopes are stretches of concrete wall that mark the various *domaines*, or *mas*, and carry the proprietors' names in letters four feet high. In winter, Hermitage bristles with the tall stakes that support each vine, but from late spring onwards, the whole hillside is clothed in green, "changed by every slide or stroke of wind like the ruffled nap of velvet"—John Arlott's evocative words.

Gérard Chave, in his mid-forties, is totally charming, but verges on the fanatical in his obsession with the quality of his wine. The last independent grower on the hillside to make and bottle his own Hermitage, Gérard is the latest in the succession of Chave fathers and sons to have owned the best-exposed vineyard of all since 1481. Its gradient is so steep that Gérard has devised his own system for the harvest. A small petrol engine hauls a stout sledge up a sort of *piste* between the vines, so that the grape-filled *bennes*, wooden tubs, can be lowered to the gentler slopes below. Each *benne* has a projecting lug at either side, under which poles are placed. These are shouldered by two men who thus carry the tub to the waiting trailer, sedan chair fashion.

On the last day of the 1972 *récolte*, we saw Gerard's perfectionism in action. The pickers, most of whom have worked for the Chaves for years, were leaving what appeared to be healthy, ripe grapes on the vines. Good they were, but not good enough to meet Gérard's exacting requirements, as the *vendangeurs* well knew. They were to be left for the birds or village boys. As the last trailer-load of *bennes* was about to leave for the Chave cellars at Mauves, a sudden shower of rain passed over. Without a word, the personnel doffed their jackets and spread them over the tubs; they themselves might get wet, but the grapes, never.

The same care is taken when the grapes arrive at the cellars behind and below the Chave's house in Mauves. After pressing, the juice ferments in nine foot high one hundred year old wooden vats. The skins and pips rise to the surface as a dense crust, the *chapeau*. For the next four or five days the *chapeau* is trodden down twice daily, by foot, into the fermenting juice, so that the new wine will be rich in body and tannin. The wine is kept in oak barrel for at least two years, the traditional ageing in wood. The quality of Gérard Chave's Hermitage reflects his skill and intensive, obsessive devotion; it is fine, dark and perfectly balanced, with potential to become a wonderfully complex, deeply satisfying, almost revelatory experience. Patience is needed for the wine to reach this point of perfection, however, as Hermitage may take as long as fifteen or twenty years to reach full maturity. Last year at our favourite Michelin three-star restaurant, *Pic* in Valence, we watched with sadness as twenty or more bottles of Gérard's marvellous 1976 vintage were poured down uncomprehending French throats—sheer infanticide!

Gérard makes his white Hermitage with exactly the same care as the red, from the traditional white grapes of the region, the *marsanne* and *roussanne*. Old style white Hermitage was famous for its staying power, and was said to have remained potable for many years. We have tasted an example of the 1929 vintage, and indeed it was drinkable: just. Once a sought-after style of wine, we doubt that that dark-yellow, almost brown, heavy, oxidised sort of wine has much appeal nowadays. We ourselves infinitely prefer the white Hermitage that Gérard makes today. Rather than keep the wine in wood for two years or more, as tradition dictated, he now bottles in the spring following the vintage, thus conserving all the zest and freshness and fruitiness of the young wine.

CROZES HERMITAGE

Vineyards that lie to either side and behind the hill of Hermitage have the *appellation* of Crozes Hermitage. Quality can vary considerably, according to soil constitution and exposure to the sun.

The small village of Gervans is three kilometres north of Tain l'Hermitage, just off the RN7, the old main arterial road from Paris to Marseilles. The vineyards that surround the village are considered to be the source of the best Crozes Hermitage. Raymond Roure lives high above Gervans; his house can only be reached by mounting the escarpment by a series of hairpin bends. That his wines, both red and white, are reputed throughout the region is due to Raymond's skill as a *vigneron* and to the startling steepness of his vineyard. On such a gradient each individual vine receives maximum benefit from direct exposure to the sun throughout the day. The Roure grapes ripen earlier than those of his colleagues in the village below, and more fully, but at a cost. The difficulty of the various vineyard operations, the *taillage*, or pruning, in January, the tying and retying to supporting stakes at frequent intervals throught the summer, the spraying of the vines with chemical preparations and pesticides five or six times during the growing season and, finally, the harvest, or *récolte*, all these represent enormous extra effort and labour on such an incline. For Raymond Roure the struggle is justified by the results that he achieves, for he makes a fine, powerful wine that can only be distinguished from those made on the hill of Hermitage itself by the exercise of considerable concentration, and discernment learned from long experience.

CORNAS

At Cornas, the *syrah* makes a dark, dark, powerful wine with a potential longevity similar to that of its famous neighbour, Hermitage. Perhaps fractionally less elegant than Hermitage, Cornas is a little more *corsé*— a near-untranslatable word that implies an almost aggressive full-bodied-ness. The vineyards, ten kilometres south of Tournon and Tain, run west from the level terrain beside the RN86 onto the steep slopes of the foothills of the Ardèche, where all work must necessarily be manual. The hills afford welcome protection against the chilly blast of the *mistral*, and the grapes ripen earlier than those of Hermitage. Less fortunate is the district's attraction as a dormitory for nearby Valence: the area under vines decreases annually as urbanisation creeps nearer.

It is no surprise to us that Auguste Clape has achieved a wide recognition throughout France, and further, since our first purchase ten years ago. We have remained fervent admirers of his fine wine ever since our first taste. John Livingstone-Learmonth and Melvyn Master, in their emotive "Wines of the Rhône", describe Auguste as "Cornas's best-known grower and the one who makes the best wine." Such approbation leads to an increased demand, and as his nine acres produce around ten thousand bottles in an average year, often less, it becomes increasingly difficult to abstract a sufficient quantity from the small Clape cellar. We are privileged to receive an allocation of between 5 and 10% of his annual production. The most traditional of all growers at Cornas, Auguste still uses an old-fashioned hydraulic press, ferments the juice for twelve days—not the speeded-up five or six day affair of more commercial

Château de Crussol

producers—and matures the wine in oak casks from Gevrey Chambertin
for at least two years. After such care, it seems only just that the eventual
consumer should be prepared to keep such a wine for five years, or,
counsel of perfection, much longer.

SAINT PÉRAY

The small but lively town of Saint Péray is immediately to the south of Cornas, facing the rapidly expanding city of Valence across the Rhône. Dramatic limestone crags rise behind the town, capped by the ruins of Château de Crussol, the chief landmark of the area. Wine has been made at Saint Péray for more than two thousand years, being mentioned by both Pliny and Plutarch. Until the discovery of the *méthode champenoise* by Dom Perignon in the seventeenth century, only a still white wine, Saint Péray *nature*, was made from the two white grapes of the Northern Rhône, the *roussanne* and the *marsanne*. The Duke of Wellington was invited to assay the *nature* in London on 23 July, 1822, being told by his host that it was 'a very pretty wine . . . Saint Pery.' The Duke tasted it, and then said "Perry! My God! but how it got sainted I can't guess." Vinification must have improved somewhat in the intervening fifty years as, in December 1877, Richard Wagner, whilst composing Parsifal, wrote from Bayreuth to urge the dispatch of a hundred bottles at the earliest opportunity.

Nowadays only one-fifth of the production is of the still wine, the rest being fully sparkling. The growers insist that it was Dom Perignon himself who made the first batch of Saint Péray *mousseux*, whilst visiting the region. Certainly the technique is exactly as that employed in Champagne, even to the use of the same yeasts. By the middle of the nineteenth century the sparkling wine had assumed considerable commercial importance, being a favourite in Victorian England. The smaller growers have united to form a small *coopérative*, and make their *mousseux* in extensive cellars below the rather strange *Hôtel des Bains*. Jean-François Chaboud (with twenty acres, a major grower), has his own cellars behind the rue Ferdinand-Mallett, where he uses 60% *marsanne* with 40% *roussanne* to produce a pale-golden wine, richer and fruitier than Champagne, that is at its best after three to four years in bottle. His delicious *nature* has similar characteristics, but ages even better.

CLAIRETTE DE DIE

Another sparkling wine region lies sixty kilometres to the south-east of Saint Péray, where the turbulent River Drôme cascades through the gorges of the first outcroppings of the mountains of the Alps. Vines grow beside the river on each side of the mountain town of Die. The road from Valence hugs the course of the Drôme. After Crest (where the restaurant *Kléber* serves pleasant food at reasonable cost, including a local speciality, *Défarde Crestoise*—a sort of *pieds et pacquets*) the scenery becomes wilder and more impressive. The peaks of *Les Trois Becs* tower above the valley, retaining their snow caps until early summer. Just seven kilometres before Die, Sainte Croix appears ahead, the tiny hamlet perched above the rushing waters of the Drôme. Here M. Vincent (the Frachet came with his wife and her dowry, or *dot*, of vineyards) has his walnut plantations and five acres of vines. His dry, sparkling wine, crisp and refreshing, is made entirely from the *Clairette* by the *méthode champenoise*. Pleasanter, and better value than many of the dubious "real" champagnes that are perpetrated on an unsuspecting public even more in France than in England, the *brut*, or dry Clairette-de-Die has proved a great success for the region, since it was first produced commercially in the early 1960's.

However, the truly distinctive wine of the region is the *demi-sec* Clairette-de-Die *naturel*, made by the unique *méthode Dieoise*, which has captivated a large proportion of our customers. M. Vincent uses 30% *Clairette* and, for the region, the relatively high proportion of 70% *muscat* to produce his flowery, gorgeously fragrant Clairette-de-Die *naturel*, which has the unmistakable aroma and taste of the *muscat* grape. The *méthode Dieoise* involves slowing down fermentation by monthly filtering, thus removing the largest yeast cells, until the wine is bottled in the January or February following the vintage. Sufficient natural sugar and yeast remains to cause secondary fermentation within the bottle, so the wine is veritably *naturel*. After nine months in bottle, the wine is decanted, filtered for the last time, and rebottled. We have enjoyed many bottles of Clairette-de-Die *naturel* ever since our first visit to Sainte Croix, but no bottle has been more memorable than the first, consumed with a picnic high up on the *Col de la Chaudière*, the vertiginous pass below *Les Trois Becs*, en route to Tricastin and the southern Côtes du Rhône.

TRICASTIN

East of Montélimar and Bollène lies what was once a thriving, prosperous viticultural area. Until the scourge of phylloxera killed the vines here, as everywhere else in France, in the 1880's, the wine was considered the equal of Châteauneuf-du-Pape. Thereafter the economy, such as it was, depended on small, isolated farmsteads surrounded by an encroaching wilderness of gorse and thorn, pines and scrubby oak trees. Ultimately the only fame of Tricastin rested in its valuable subterranean resource, the truffle. Even today, one sees small groups of local men in village streets each Saturday morning, examining and trading their "black diamonds".

At the time of the Algerian Revolution, the dispossessed French colonialists, *pieds noirs*, returned to France with whatever funds they had been able to salvage, and looked around for suitable employment. Those who had owned extensive vineyards in Algeria found that existing vineyards, if available at all, were very costly. An enterprising few deduced the potential of Tricastin. Among them were Henri Bour and his wife, both descendants of important wine dynasties. In 1964 they bought the crumbling shell of a farmhouse and fifty acres of what to all appearances was barren and unpromising terrain near the village of Roussas. The Bours laboriously grubbed out the trees and bushes, removed the boulders, to create eventually an immaculate vineyard. The pioneering efforts of people like the Bours have restored the region to something like its former eminence, and the wine they make has found deserved recognition. Tricastin has risen from being a *Vin de Table* to

[87]

V.D.Q.S., to full *appellation* within fifteen years; a remarkable achievement.

Domaine de Grangeneuve, the Bour estate, is now an impressive place. Vintage-time there presents as unusual a sight as any we know. While the level parts are harvested by an enormous *machine à vendanger*, mechanical reaper, the vines on the slopes are being systematically picked by a group of Cistercian monks from a nearby abbey. No matter the method by which the grapes are gathered, Henri Bour's expert vinification produces a most pleasing wine, full, soft and fruity.

CÔTES DU VENTOUX

Mont Ventoux rises from the surrounding plain and hills in magnificent grandeur. Snow covers its summit until late spring, and a small ski station attracts winter sportsmen from all over France. We have found it somewhat bizarre in April to breakfast outdoors at Vaison-la-Romaine in the warm provençal sun, and, later in the morning, ascend above the snowline of Ventoux to behold the busy ski slopes. Lower on the mountain, vines grow in any possible situation, any pocket of soil that has good exposure to the sun. The wine, Côtes du Ventoux, is a light, fragrant red, its delicate colour belying the depth and interest of its flavour. The growers were ecstatic when Côtes du Ventoux was elevated to *appellation* status in 1972. The climax of their joyous celebrations was a general price increase of fifty centimes per bottle.

CÔTES DU RHÔNE

Generic Côtes du Rhône wines can vary considerably in style and standard. Of the hundreds available, the following three offer particularly high quality and interest.

Puyméras is a quiet village, hidden in the hills to the north-east of Vaison-la-Romaine. An attractive provençal fountain splashes near the covered washpool; a large plane tree gives welcome shade in summer, and a wooden board tacked to its trunk indicates the *boulangerie*. Amazingly, the wine of Puyméras is little known, even in its own region. As it is particularly good, this must be attributable to the inaccessibility of the village. The *Cave Vinicole*, founded in 1930, is in some ways anachronistic in its methods and attitudes. This probably stems from the conviction of its forceful director, Pierre Audibert, that short cuts, accelerated methods of vinification or high commercialism are not wanted at Puyméras. Ninety per cent of the *Cave's* wine is sold in bulk to *negoçiants*, and at least some of it probably finds its way north to Burgundy. Only the wine of the good years is bottled. The vineyards are at a higher altitude than elsewhere, which may be a factor in the exceptional fruitiness and higher than usual tannin content of the red wine. After a long fermentation, Puyméras is kept in wood for a year, then another in bottle—an almost-unique holding operation for a Côtes du Rhône. The wine that results is *costaud*; strapping, muscular, a wine of strong character that is enjoyable immediately, but that will repay a few years keeping.

If anything, the white wine is even more unusual. A lot of white Côtes du Rhônes are over-endowed with alcohol, so rather flabby and uninteresting. White Puyméras, which forms a mere ½% of total production, is the reverse, being a delicious, zestful, tasty wine.

Christian Favier has his vines at Travaillan, on the vast *Plan de Dieu*, betwen Orange and Gigondas. His wine, La Pousaranque, differs hugely from the other wines of the *Plan*. The secret lies in its vinification. Christian had the good sense to marry Marie-Paul, the elder daughter of (in our opinion) the best wine maker at Châteauneuf-du-Pape, Noël Sabon. The grapes are brought the sixteen kilometres to the Sabon cellars, and it is Noël who helps Christian to vinify the juice. La Pousaranque is dark and elegant, with an individual character that indicates the need to mature it for several years, even for so long as five or six. Indeed, so good is the wine, so firmly imprinted is it with Noël Sabon's style, that it regularly forms one of the minor hazards of buying trips. Tasting the *cuves* of Chante Cigale is a strange, ritualistic affair. We sit in state in armchairs in the Sabons' *salon*, plastic cellar buckets at our sides, whilst the samples, *échantillons*, are solemnly brought to us from the cellar. The Sabon family stand by, dearly wishing us to fail in detecting Christian's wine, concealed somewhere among the two dozen bottles. We have always succeeded in spotting it, so far . . .

It has been our mission during the last ten years to persuade our customers to keep their red Rhône wines until they have acquired the virtue that comes with age and maturity. M. Pascal's well-made, medal-winning Côtes du Rhône has been aged in his cellars at Vacqueyras, and exemplifies the characteristics of a mature red wine.

GIGONDAS AND VACQUEYRAS

The sense of being in Provence grows stronger on the drive south to Orange, more so on the old RN7 than the autoroute. The low farmhouses begin to be roofed with curved terra cotta tiles, as since Roman times. Clumps of cypress trees are glimpsed, olive groves, dense thickets of tall bamboos, planted as windbreaks when, suddenly, away to the east, there looms up the huge, dominant landmark of all this part of Provence, Mont Ventoux. The RN7 enters Orange by the *Arc de Triomphe*, only one of the Roman monuments in the town. Orange has a truly provençal feel. On market days the narrow streets are impassable to motorcars, being completely blocked by people and stalls, including that of the olive woman. By the towering facade of the Roman amphitheatre she vends fish preserved in brine, *cornichons*, gherkins, and a dozen or more varieties of olives, green and black, from huge terra cotta pots.

Driving east, crossing the wide plain, the *Plan De Dieu*, Mont Ventoux gradually becomes obscured by its own foothills. Amazing, dramatic limestone crags emerge from steep slopes of dense woodland, cork oaks and pines, to claw the clear blue sky—the beautiful *Dentelles de Montmirail*. A cluster of ochre-coloured cottages halfway up the slope represent the village of Gigondas. The red wine of Gigondas has always been one of the darkest, richest and most powerful of all the southern Côtes-du-Rhône. In 1971 its consistently high quality resulted in the granting of a separate *appellation*: a recognition otherwise only granted to Châteauneuf-du-Pape and to Lirac. Domaine Saint Gayan consists of thirty-eight acres of prime vineyard, albeit stony, along the Gigondas-

Sablet border. Here perhaps the most serious of the dozen or so individual growers of the *commune* grows his vines and makes his marvellous wine. Roger Meffre could be called *maniaque*—a not impolite French word that signifies intense single-minded enthusiasm to a cause. Roger's obsession is to make the finest wine in Gigondas every single year, and to that end his devotion is absolute. He relies on the bulk sale of the generic Côtes-du-Rhône that he produces at Sablet for general income. This means that Roger Meffre can afford to pick only the best, most perfect, fully ripe grapes for his Gigondas, and to use the *méthode ancienne*. The *fouloir*, a sort of crushing mangle, is set to a wider aperture than at other domaines, so that many grapes pass through whole. After a long fermentation, the new wine is drawn off, to leave the lees, or *marc*, containing the same whole grapes, whose juice has fermented anaerobically. The *marc* is gently pressed in an ancient hydraulic *pressoir*, and the juice added to the first-made wine. After a year in cement *cuve*, and two more in oak barrel, the wine is fined with egg albumen, and bottled without filtration. Roger has again come up with a huge, dark, strong wine, the best in Gigondas, with a rich colour and a lot of tannin, a wine that can mature in bottle for many years. No wonder that Domaine Saint Gayan invariably receives the gold medal at the *Concours Agricole*, and that those of us privileged enough to get an allocation each year would very much like to be able to purchase more.

The Meffre *rosé* is no less carefully made. The same *fouloir* semi-crushes 50% grenache and 25% each of *clairette* and *cinsault*. The bruised grapes and juice rest together for less than twenty-four hours. When Roger judges that the mélange has acquired exactly the degree of colouration that he deems ideal, the juice, the *tête de cuvée* is removed and made into his elegant but alcoholic Gigondas *rosé*. The grapes have not been pressed, and thereafter the wine is never in contact with wood. Its freshness and fruitiness are best conserved by using enamel *cuves* only.

Further south, three kilometres round the *Dentelles*, the vineyards of Vacqueyras are guarded by a walled village of the same name. The stout walls and crenellated gateways vividly remind the visitor that life was not always so tranquil and unhurried in these parts.

With very similar characteristics to the wine of its better known neighbour, Vacqueyras is only fractionally less impressive. Regarded as one of the best of the Côtes-du-Rhône *villages*, that *appellation* in itself indicates that the wine is a good cut above a generic Côtes-du-Rhône. We list a Vacqueyras of the splendid 1976 vintage, made by Monsieur Pascal, who established his business on the road between Gigondas and Vacqueyras eleven years ago. M. Pascal, who has a similar enterprise in Burgundy, is a *vinificateur*, an expert maker of wine, and himself owns no vines. His function is to be very, very selective in the buying of the best possible grapes of each of the local *communes* at the time of the harvest, and then to employ his undoubted skill in producing superb examples of those wines. That he amply succeeds is clearly attested by the frequency with which the Pascal wines are awarded medals at the important Rhône Wine Fair held each January in Orange.

MUSCAT DE BEAUMES-DE-VENISE

Six kilometres south of Gigondas, the small town of Beaumes-de-Venise, a jumble of golden-yellow houses and cottages surmounted by the grey ruins of the château, sprawls on the steep slope of the farther side of the *Dentelles de Montmirail*. The centre of Beaumes is marked by a splendid provençal fountain and a busy bar-restaurant, the *Lou Castelet*. Here the accommodation is simple and cheap, the food good, and the atmosphere welcoming. The vineyard workers gather in the bar after their day's toil to converse, to play a curious local dice game, and to take an apéritif before their evening meal. Our theory that, whilst the French make the best wines in the world, it is the English who best know how to consume them, is upheld here in Beaumes. That golden-amber liquid in each glass is the most important product of the town, the gorgeous, tangy, flavoursome Muscat de Beaumes-de-Venise. The men who make it drink the wine as a precursor to a meal, not, as any self-respecting Englishmen would know by instinct, as a dessert wine. The road from Gigondas to Carpentras, the D7, skirts Beaumes to the west. Here, near the landmark of the church tower of Notre Dame d'Aubune, the *Cave Coopérative* was built in 1956. The *Cave* makes a delightful and consistent example of Muscat de Beaumes-de-Venise. The director, M. Paulo, will enthusiastically explain the problems of its vinification, and demonstrate the meticulous care with which it is made. The *muscat à petits-grains* is picked in October when fully ripe. The rich, tawny colour of the *Cave's* muscat results from the inclusion of 5% of black grapes. Rich in sugar (they must have at least two hundred and fifty-two grammes per litre of

[97]

juice) they are de-stalked in the *égrappoir*, and pressed. The juice passes through a cooling machine, to enter the concrete *cuves* at 0°C. Fermentation takes ten or twelve days, during which the temperature rises to 10—12°C, and any solid matter sinks to the bottom of the tank. The next stage, the *mutage*, is crucial. At precisely the right moment, when the newly-formed wine has one hundred and twenty-five grammes of sugar per litre, fermentation must be arrested by the addition of 97° alcohol in exactly the correct proportion. The end result, a powerful wine with an intense fragrance that is almost pungent, and a formidable 21° of alcohol, is sealed into ornately moulded botles with metal screwtops. These are sensible, as the contents of a part-used botle will not deteriorate for several weeks, especially if kept in a refrigerator. The *Cave Coopérative* makes other wines, including a sparkling Muscat, made by the *cuve close* method, that is no match for Clairette-de-Die *naturel*. The *Cave's* boiled sweets with a liquid muscat filling are rather special, however.

Domaine de Durban is extremely difficult to locate. After an hour and more spent searching the hills in the direction of Mont Ventoux, we eventually found the track that mounts for three kilometres into the *Dentelles de Montmirail*. High on a plateau hidden in the hills is the impressive estate of Jacques Leydier. He is one of the mere handful of growers who kept alive the making of traditional Muscat between the two World Wars. Until the grant of *appellation* in 1945, M. Leydier and his friends would pick the fully-ripe grapes in mid-October and lay them on straw mats to ripen further before pressing. The more controllable method employed today must make his life relatively easier, and the Leydiers seem to make a splendid wine every year.

In Roman times, the discovery of a sulphur spring led to the establishment of a small spa, called Urban—hence the modern name. As recently as the last century at least seventy people lived here, but now all that remains is the Leydiers' fine house. At such an altitude, water supply is a problem. The ancient cistern, or reservoir, of the former village forms part of the house, and is still of tremendous value during the long, hot provençal summer. More amazing yet, the *cuverie* below the elegant sitting room was the subterranean chapel of the small community, as the

[98]

vaulted roof and tiny gothic window high in one wall testify. The chapel is now devoted to the secular ceremony of the vinification of the Leydiers' transcendental wine. At an altitude of four hundred and forty metres, Jacques' vines are less beset by the maladies to which the *muscat* is notoriously prone than those of his less fortunate colleagues on the plain below. Only white grapes, *grains-blancs*, are used to form the green-gold miracle of Durban. Even the charming and intelligent Leydiers, makers of such nectar (in our opinion, comparable with the best dessert wines of the Sauternais or Loire) will still offer you their superb product as an apéritif. They are prepared, however, to concede the wine's valuable place as the appropriate termination of a fine repast and, further, to urge their clients to conserve the wine. The Leydiers feel that twenty years should not be too long to wait for eventual reflective and reverential enjoyment, though we think that they realise that a lot of us are appreciating their wine right now.

Domaine de Durban

CHÂTEAUNEUF-DU-PAPE

Châteauneuf-du-Pape is the best known of all the wines of the southern Côtes-du-Rhône. Logically so, as it is undoubtedly the finest, having an extraordinary depth of flavour and a finesse that surpasses that of Gigondas. The enormous fame of Châteauneuf must stem from something even more than its sheer quality. Perhaps it is easier to pronounce than other vineyard names. More probably, it is the romance of the sound, Châteauneuf-du-Pape, conjuring up a vision of the splendid Summer Palace of the Popes, set high above the small town, surrounded by the hot, dusty, shimmering plain of Provence. The maximum planting permitted under *appellation* has brought the vineyard area to just over seven thousand five hundred acres, making Châteauneuf one of the largest *communes* in the whole Rhône. Even the volume produced from an area like this is insufficient to satisfy world demand. Far more Châteauneuf-du-Pape is sold and drunk than could possibly emanate from the *vignoble*. Obviously, a frighteningly high proportion of so-called Châteauneuf is something else or may at best be Châteauneuf stretched with an inferior wine. All of us are likely to have suffered such a Châteauneuf, and to have found it unworthy of the name, if not downright disagreeable. The genuine well-made article can be a revelation. Our first taste of Chante Cigale eight or nine years ago proved to be just such an illuminating experience. Quite simply, Noël Sabon's was and remains the best Châteauneuf-du-Pape that we have ever tasted.

In the early 1920's, the growers imposed upon themselves a rigorous system of rules, all designed to raise and then maintain the quality of the then all too often imperfect wines. The scheme, which had been instigated by the late Baron Le Roy of Château Fortia, proved to be extremely successful. In 1936 the laws were used as the basis of a national method of viticultural standard control and called *Appellation d'Origine Controlée*, or A.O.C., to be administered from Paris by a governing body, the I.N.A.O., the *Institut National d'Appellation d'Origine*. The first *appellation* was granted, naturally enough, to Châteauneuf-du-Pape. In the years following, more and more areas were able to meet the exacting requirements needed for similar recognition.

As many as thirteen types of vine are permitted to be grown at Châteauneuf, but in fact each grower selects only those vines that experience has shown to produce the best results on his type of soil. Only the *syrah* can be supported on wire, the other varieties being grown as widely separated self-supporting bushes.

French laws of inheritance tend to result in the fragmentation of originally larger estates as they are equally divided between the offspring at each succession. Generations of marriage settlements can similarly lead to the accumulation of a number of small properties. Noël Sabon's vines are randomly scattered in this way, and his seventy acres are split into twenty-five different portions, inconveniently situated in all parts of the *commune*. In one place he owns a row and a half of vines, there being no physical indication of where the part row becomes the property of a neighbour. Fortunately, border disputes seem to be rare, if they exist at all. Elsewhere, a stretch of fifteen acres forms another part of the Sabon *domaine*. In some parts the soil is entirely concealed by huge, round stones, and the wonder is that the vines can grow at all. The stones reflect the heat of the hot provençal sun back onto the grapes during the day, and release stored-up heat at night. Thus, the grapes are more fully ripened and have a higher sugar content, so that the wine will be strong. By law Châteauneuf must have a minimum alcohol level of 12.5°, the highest such requirement for a natural red wine in France, but more usually it has a heady 13.5—14.5°. Chante Cigale is generally made with 80% *grenache*, 12% *syrah*, 5% *mourvèdre* and a little *cinsault*, although the blend will be subtly adjusted in particular years. The sudden onset of the fierce, cold

Rhône wind, the *mistral*, can lower the air temperature abruptly, and affect the process of fermentation. Noël Sabon has installed expensive stainless steel *cuves*, the temperature of which can be exactly controlled to an ideal 18—20°, the *mistral* notwithstanding. Thus fermentation can proceed without hitch for the required fifteen to twenty-one days.

Thereafter the wine is kept in huge oak barrels for at least two years, usually longer. It seems that Noël is the last *vigneron* at Châteauneuf-du-Pape to adhere to such traditional methods, which must be the secret of his marvellous wine. Chante Cigale is rich, dark and powerful, a wine of great elegance and enormous distinction.

TAVEL AND LIRAC

The neighbouring villages of Tavel and Lirac lie somewhat hidden in the *garrigue*, or stony, hilly scrubland, ten kilometres west of Châteauneuf-du-Pape and fifteen kilometres north-west of Avignon. Both vignobles make a pretty, coral-coloured wine, but Tavel has gained the reputation of being the finest *rosé* made in France and therefore, say the French, in the world. To our mind, there are other strong contenders for the title, other fine *rosés* such as Sancerre *rosé* and Pinot Gris from the Loire, or Gigondas *rosé*, or Bandol *rosé*—the staple summer beverage of the Côte d'Azur. Be that as it may, the *rosé* of Tavel and its peer, Lirac, are utterly delicious—and deceptively strong. Often recommended as an ideal accompaniment to summer picnics, their 12—13° of alcohol, in combination with hot sun, can make them exceedingly soporific—in their very quaffability and apparent innocence lies considerable danger . . .

There has been intense rivalry between the two *communes* for many years. With some justification, the growers of Lirac consider their less famous *rosé* to be the equal of Tavel. They can see no reason why the same amount of work and worry should result in less remuneration. The gaining of an *appellation* for a red Lirac has helped to salve their wounded pride. Indeed, the soft yet fullish-bodied wine, made from *grenache*, *syrah*, *mourvèdre* and *cinsault*, has achieved such success that it is the turn of Tavel to look somewhat enviously at Lirac, with a desire to make a similar red wine. Armand Maby, of Tavel, can afford to feel superior to this controversy—he has considerable holdings in the two *communes*, and has recently bought more land in each. At Tavel he has grubbed out the

[103]

scrubby oaks and pine trees from the potentially valuable slopes, near the disused phosphate mines to the west, and the young vines are growing apace.

We have a particular admiration for Armand's range of wines. His Tavel consistently wins medals at the *Concours Agricole* in Paris, as do his Lirac wines, and it epitomises the subtle, sinewy character of the famous *rosé*. In 1978 he made a Tavel *primeur*: the restaurants of the region and their clients were delighted. Our reservation would be that what the *primeur* gained in liveliness and fruit it perhaps lost in staying power, not that there is any virtue in keeping the more definitive wine for longer than two to three years. The Maby Lirac *rosé* may have subtle differences from the Tavel, but it would be an extremely skilled taster who could differentiate between them at a "blind" tasting. With similar soil, identical exposure to the sun, and exactly the same vinification of the same *cépages*, there is no reason why any great differences should exist. Being slightly the cheaper, Lirac *rosé* is perhaps the better buy.

Red Lirac is softer and lighter than the wines made further east, such as Vacqueyras and Gigondas. As such, it is enjoyable to drink at an earlier stage, after even less than a year in bottle. However, it is worth waiting longer, as five or six years of maturation produce a marked beneficial effect.

On our first visit to the Maby cellars, next to the stone and marble yard on the road to Lirac, we were astonished to discover a white Lirac, a *Blanc de Blancs* with full *appellation* status. More amazing was that this rounded, fruity and utterly delicious wine had never been mentioned in any wine book that we had ever read. Less than 4% of Lirac is made as white, but we are encouraging Armand to devote some of his new land to its production.

A tasting *chez* Maby is always of interest. It is particularly instructive to taste the *cuves* of the separate *cépages*—pure *syrah*, undiluted *grenache*, 100% *mourvèdre*, et cetera. One begins to comprehend the significance of, for example, *mourvèdre* in the eventual blend, its resistance to oxidation giving the wine a longer life.

In January 1979, when the vineyards were too muddy for the pruning, or *taillage*, to continue, the workers were building an elegant tasting hall and a wine library, where stone bins will eventually hold one thousand four hundred bottles of each good vintage. The Maby establishment will be certainly worth a visit (or *vaut un détour*, as M. Michelin says) when those bottles have had an opportunity to mature. The small, charming, ancient *Hostellerie du Seigneur* in the centre of Tavel will make you comfortable after your tasting, and feed you generously.

COTEAUX D'AIX-EN-PROVENCE

The vineyards of Coteaux d'Aix-en-Provence are to be found in the hills above the river Durance, twenty kilometres north of the lovely city of Aix-en-Provence. Marcel Lafforgues, another ex-Algerian grower, has painstakingly created a fine vineyard from seventy acres of rough woodland near the market town of Le Puy Sainte Reparade. M. Lafforgues is a fanatical seeker of perfection with one or two rather strange notions. One such is a belief that his wine would be bruised if subjected to the pressure of a pump (as used by all other growers in the world). For this reason, the *cuverie* of Domaine de la Tour Campanets is absolutely unique. It is a tall tower, designed specially so that the grapes may enter at the top, and thereafter pass to each successive stage by gravity alone. Whether this contributes or not, Marcel Lafforgues undoubtedly makes an extremely good wine that regularly collects the gold medal at the *Concours Agricole.*

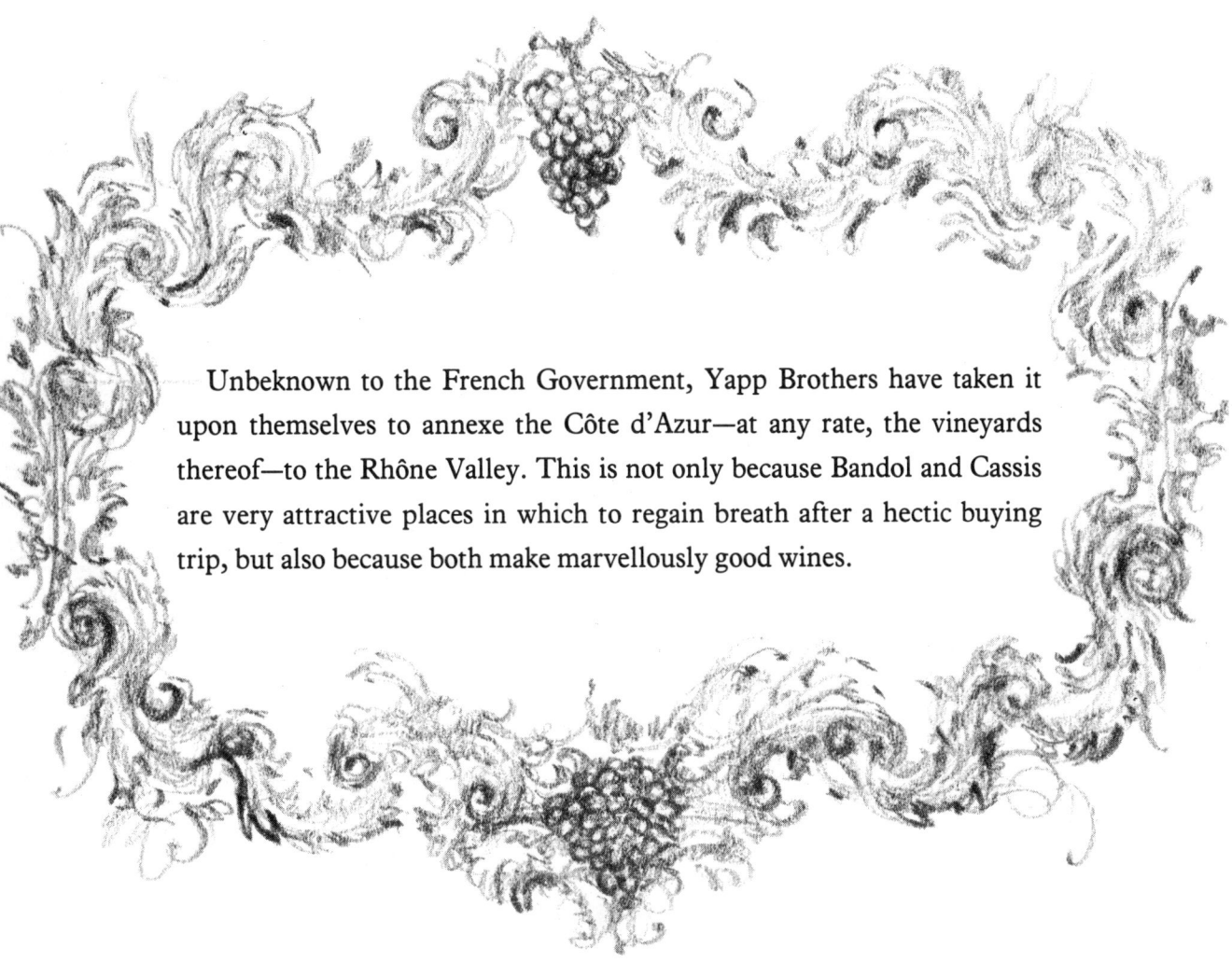

Unbeknown to the French Government, Yapp Brothers have taken it upon themselves to annexe the Côte d'Azur—at any rate, the vineyards thereof—to the Rhône Valley. This is not only because Bandol and Cassis are very attractive places in which to regain breath after a hectic buying trip, but also because both make marvellously good wines.

CASSIS

Approaching on the autoroute from Aix-en-Provence, there is a sudden glimpse of the blue Mediterranean far below, and of the Bay of Cassis. Cassis is a charming, picturesque fishing port-resort where the more successful gangsters of Marseilles have their discreet, luxurious abodes. We are normally there in January, when all is quiet and peaceful. Only the myriad shuttered fish restaurants clustered around the tiny harbour, and the ranks of tarpaulin-shrouded excursion boats among the busy fishing vessels give a hint of how thronged Cassis must be in summer.

The white wine of Cassis is delightful, but wine making here is in rapid decline. The land in the circumscribed area around the town is simply too valuable to justify the growing of vines, so despite the inordinate demand for the wine, especially in those fish restaurants, the vineyards diminish annually. One only has expanded, and that minutely, in recent years, and it must be one of the loveliest vineyards in the world. Clos Sainte Magdeleine is tucked away down the quiet Avenue de Revestel, a long cul-de-sac opposite the new casino. The neat rows of old vines and the green lawns and pines of an "English Garden" jut out as a peninsula into the azure sea. The immense, sheer face of Cap Canaille soars up from the sea to form a breathtaking backdrop. Clos Sainte Magdeleine is an exquisite, tranquil sanctuary from the bustle of the town.

François Sack, a bearded young enthusiast, shrugs his shoulders and is philosophical about the diminution of the *vignoble*. He, for his own part, has every intention of making his delicious dry, tangy, pale-topaz wine for many years to come.

BANDOL

The vineyards of Bandol lie several kilometres behind the smart, palm tree-lined esplanade and the busy marina. In happy contrast to nearby Cassis, the *vignoble* has prospered and expanded in recent years.

Paul Bunan, and his brother Pierre, were more realistic than most of the French estate owners in Algeria. Immediately after the Revolution they negotiated a sale to the new government rather than delay to be compulsorily nationalised as were others with less foresight. The Bunans astutely judged that the then little-known *vignoble* of Bandol had rich potential. They purchased a tree-clad, boulder strewn hillside in the hinterland, and proceeded to dynamite away the stone, haul out the trees and bulldoze terraces from the virgin terrain. Vines were planted, an impressively efficient press house built, and the Bunans were back in the business of making fine wine. And fine it is; we have no hesitation in counting the Bunans' red Bandol among the most splendid wines that we list. Furthermore, it shares with Châteauneuf-du-Pape and Gigondas the considerable advantage of being a plump, full-bodied generous wine that can give immediate pleasure, but will happily age and improve in bottle for, say, five to eight years. Those of our customers who have assayed red Mas de la Rouvière appear to be as enamoured of it as we; re-orders are frequent.

We find it astonishing that, with a red wine of such calibre in their cellars, the Bunans sell twice as much of their *rosé*. The pattern of their commerce explains the somewhat bizarre ratio. Every decent restaurant and hotel within the triangle formed by Marseilles, Aix and Cannes lists the Bunans' wine and in summer the majority of the vast army of tourists that fill that triangle are avid to drink the *rosé* of the region. Even the British, who are notoriously unimpressed by pink wine, might be delighted with such a delicious, vibrant characterful wine as Bandol *rosé*.

Paul Bunan

SPIRITS

SPIRITS

Drive through any small village or town in a vineyard area of France and, with some luck, you may see a weird Heath-Robinson sort of contraption in the market place. Quite probably, steam will be emerging from a copper dome amidships, and smoke rising from a tall chimney stack. You will have stumbled upon a *distillerie ambulante*, or mobile distillery. The *bouilleur de cru*, custodian of this antiquated museum piece and keeper of its secrets, is likely to be stacking the furnace at the front with coal or faggots of wood. He is in the process of distilling spirits, *eau-de-vie* or *marc*, for the local *vignerons*. It is a sight that is not likely to exist for very much longer. Growers with permits for a small annual allowance (twenty litres of 50° alcohol) cannot hand them on to their children, and no new licences are issued. Before long this endearing traditional scene will be a thing of the past.

The dense mass of skins and pips that remains after the wine has fermented is called the *marc*, as is the spirit distilled from it. Seemingly desiccated, sufficient alcohol adheres to the skins to justify distillation. The furnace heats a water tank, from which steam passes through the *marc* stacked in the central dome. The remaining alcohol is carried away in the steam, to be condensed and precipitated out in the cooling coil of the retort. Periodically, the *bouilleur* opens up the dome to remove the steaming pulp and replace it with a fresh supply.

Marc has a highly individual grapy taste. *Eau-de-vie*, usually a smoother, less aggressive spirit, is distilled from any alcoholic liquid, be it wine or any other fermented fruit juice. A travelling still will normally be

producing an *eau-de-vie du vin* from the sludgy lees of wine left when wine has been decanted into a fresh barrel. Occasionally a *vigneron* will come to the market place with some fruit juice, pear or perhaps plum, that he has fermented at home in advance of the *distillerie's* arrival in town. A small still parked under the chestnut trees by the church in Savennieres was producing a near-lethal potion of *Poire William* one Easter. By comparison, Jean Vatan's plum *eau-de-vie* seemed relatively innocuous, though just as freshly brewed.

The operations of a mobile *distillerie* are very much under government supervision. Taking a much-chewed pencil from behind his ear, the *bouilleur* must laboriously enter precise details of volume and strength into his official buff notebook at ten minute intervals. At the end of a distillation, the precious liquor is poured into the customer's *bonbon* (glass carboy) and the contents adjusted to the exact twenty litres at 50° by the addition of a calculated amount of pure water. The surplus alcohol falls to the state, and is destined for use as surgical spirit, or so the *bouilleur* says.

Knowing the paucity of the individual allowance, we were positively embarrassed by the generosity of a particular grower friend who insisted on sending us on our way each year, laden with several bottles of his "armagnac". When we expressed our hesitation in accepting such a gift, he laughed and reminded us that before their marriage his wife had been a laboratory technician. It had not occurred to us that the glassware in the bathroom constituted a fully operational still; we had been paying the Customs officers at Southampton duty on "bathtub armagnac".

Liqueurs, such as Crème de Cassis or Crème de Myrtilles, are made by lightly crushing the fruit and macerating it in alcohol for two months, exactly as in the domestic fabrication of sloe gin. Sloes are the basis of Prunelle. The sloes have been de-pitted and the stones washed and cleaned before they arrive at a manufactory, such as Boudier in Dijon. The sloe stones are immersed in 80° alcohol in miniature vats for several months until all the flavour has been absorbed to form a marvellously subtle liqueur. Prunelle, which has a unique taste of almonds, is the most interesting and compelling *digestif* that we have come across in a very long time.

The fields around the city of Orleans are mainly devoted to the cultivation of pear trees, all neatly pruned and tied espalier-fashion to wire supports. In springtime the sea of white blossom is incredibly lovely and the air is heavy with an overpowering fragrance. Some of the eventual fruit will be preserved by canning but most will be used to make *eau-de-vie de poire william*. The harvested fruit is macerated and left to ferment in large enamel *cuves*; the fermented juice is then distilled in the usual way. Of the many manufactories of the liquor in and around Orleans, none makes a finer *poire william* than Covifruit, a *coopérative* of small growers at Olivet, a village just south of Orleans. Their magnums of *poire william* present a perplexing riddle; each bottle contains a large, perfectly formed pear. Ingenious suggestions as to how a four inch pear may be passed through a half inch bottle neck are various, but the truth is stranger than any proffered solution. If you search through the orchards you will find a number of very strange looking pear trees festooned with bottles. When the blossom has fallen, only one embryonic fruit is allowed to develop at the tip of each branch; a bottle is slipped over the tiny pear and tied securely to the branch. A complicated and expensive caprice on the part of the growers, one might think, but on further reflection perhaps it makes more economic sense than might at first appear; after all, each pear does represent a saving of a considerable number of centilitres of precious alcohol.

CRÈME DE CASSIS

Vin Blanc Cassis has become a fashionable beverage since the last war. Perhaps better known nowadays as a Kir, it is thus named in affectionate remembrance of an enthusiastic consumer of the drink, the late Canon Felix Kir, for many years Mayor of Dijon and a hero of the *résistance*. The virtue and beneficial quality of the concoction is evidenced by the Canon's longevity: he died ten years ago at the age of ninety-two.

The recipe varies from bar to bar, person to person, but the concept remains the same. Crème de Cassis, a liqueur made from blackcurrants grown in Burgundy, is added to a dry white wine in the proportion, Yapp formula, of one to seven. A Burgundian, as likely demanding a *rince cochon* (pig wash) rather than a Kir, would prefer to go thirsty than accept any other wine in place of Bourgogne Aligoté. However, there are plenty of discerning drinkers who prefer to employ wines of somewhat higher acidity, such as Gros Plant, or Saint Pourçain, which they consider to make a more refreshing apéritif at appreciably lower cost.

We admire, revere, indeed love the witty, wise and handsome Mr. Cyril Ray. We have only once heard him express an opinion that was less than worthy. This dubious statement appeared in print: "Cyril Ray of Punch says, oh, pooh, you can use Ribena . . . and nobody will know the difference." In the two weeks following the appearance of this heretical nonsense, all unsuspecting callers at the Old Brewery were subjected to a comparative "blind" tasting of a proper Kir and a Ribena-based non-Kir. The results of this referendum were dispatched to the miscreant wine writer; a vociferous 100% vote had been cast in favour of the real, Yapp authenticated mix, and Mr. Ray had lost face. We have awaited his retraction, but so far in vain.

RIBENA!

CRÈME DE MYRTILLES

The name MYR (pronounced MERE) was coined, or more appropriately, composed by Harrison Birtwistle at his home on the small island of Raasay, just to the north of Skye. We were there for the New Year, and were occupying ourselves in doing research on a new drink that Judith and I had discovered whilst staying in the Ardèche some months earlier. Our grower friend Gérard Chave had lent us his small farmhouse, high in the mountains above the Rhône, with a spectacular view down across the river to the hill of Hermitage, where the Chaves have owned vines for as long as they have owned the farm, since 1481. One hot day in July, we took the steam train, the *Chemin de Fer du Vivarais*, from Tournon to the mountain town of Lamastre. The little engine chugged its way up into the mountains via precipice and gorge, passing the elegant single arch of the Roman bridge, Caesar's Bridge, that spans the river Doux. From the small station of Lamastre, passing through the bustling market, with the stalls of cheese factors come to buy in the goats' cheeses made by the peasant women of the area, past men selling and buying the same goats tied up in hessian sacks, a short walk brought us to the object of our expedition. The famous *Hôtel du Midi*, or *Chez Barattero*, the two-star restaurant-hotel, so evocatively and affectionately described by Elizabeth David in French Provincial Cooking, has had virtually the same menu for the twenty-five or so years since Monsieur Barattero died. The same few superb dishes have been lovingly prepared and presented by his widow and her chef each day since then, as a curious sort of memorial: *terrine de bécasse*, the fine, delicate *pain d'écrevisse, poularde en vessie* (a Bresse

[118]

chicken with slices of truffle placed under its skin, and then cooked in brandy and an aromatic stock, inside a pig's bladder) and so on. We had arranged to meet Gérard and Monique Chave at the hotel, and they duly arrived, having driven the forty kilometres of hairpin bends from Tournon.

Because we have eaten there on several occasions, old Madame Barattero now knows us. As Gérard is the best-known and most widely respected grower in the region, she knows him very well, so we were not surprised to be offered an apéritif with Mme. Barattero's compliments. Sitting in the sunshine on the terrace that juts out into the busy market square, we took our first sip of something completely new to us, something marvellous; indeed, it was a revelation. It proved to be our discovery of MYR or *Vin Blanc Myrtilles*—a drink virtually unknown in France itself. The magic ingredient is a liqueur made from *Myrtilles*, or bilberries. This is mixed with a dry, white wine to produce a delicious apéritif that we think far transcends a kir, or *Vin Blanc Cassis*, in flavour and subtlety.

However, that original Barattero version had some imperfections. For instance, the liqueur had been made from bilberry extracts, rather than fresh fruit, and the wine used had, if anything, been too dry. After several months, we succeeded in searching out a small firm of distillers in Dijon, who appear to be the only people to make a Crème de Myrtilles from fresh bilberries, La Maison Boudier. Wild bilberries gathered in the mountains of the Ardèche and the Drôme are lightly crushed and macerated for two months in pure alcohol, until all the possible flavour and colouring has been extracted, when an exactly controlled amount of sugar is added.

Our further investigation was to select the liqueur with the ideal strength of alcohol, and the most suitable white wine with which to match it. Hence our self-imposed travail on Raasay at the New Year. Whilst incidentally establishing that interesting and palatable versions can be made with red wines, and with sparkling wines, the unanimous conclusion was that 35° Crème de Myrtilles combined to perfection with a dry-ish white Loire wine, such as Saumur Blanc. Obviously, others may

choose to experiment themselves, and may well choose a somewhat different formula. Be that as it may, we are sure that MYR will become extremely popular . . . so perhaps we should ask Harrison Birtwistle to compose a television jingle immediately.

OLIVE OIL

There seems to be a fairly well-established tradition that superior wine merchants should stock an olive oil and a wine vinegar. While we would certainly never care to be thought of as less than superior wine merchants, it had never really seemed important that we should follow suit. Therefore we cannot claim too much percipience as far as our discovery of La Balméenne is concerned; the stuff simply refused to be ignored. One of the hazards of the wine trade are the afternoon-long luncheons that grower friends insist upon providing. In Provence we could not avoid noticing that the dressing of the inevitable salad was always particularly appetizing and unusually fine. Feeling rather relaxed by this stage of the proceedings, we confess that we failed miserably in what in retrospect was our evident duty—to establish the reason for the remarkable flavour. Subsequently, whilst dining at the simple restaurant in Beaumes-de-Venise, the *Lou Castelet,* we again met the self-same taste. Perhaps more alert than on previous encounters, we made enquiries that revealed the cause of this excellence. It was, of course, the quality of the olive oil. The olive oil of Provence has always been highly esteemed, the olives of Northern Provence thought to be the best, and, as our grower friends were evidently aware, the most superlative olive oil of all is made in Beaumes-de-Venise, at an old *moulin d'huile d'olive,* La Balméenne.

At nine o'clock next morning we presented ourselves at the somewhat decrepit premises, every bit of sixty yards from the *Lou Castelet.* The director was charming, happy to show us the establishment and to explain the processes involved. As with the best wines, the finest fruit

only is harvested. Large stone wheels crush the olives, which are then packed between hessian mats so that the oil may be expressed in handsome nineteenth century cast-iron presses. Most *huileries* use some form of heat to increase the yield, and the pulp may be pressed several times. At La Balméenne the one pressing is "cold", so that the oil is the purest that it is possible to obtain; it is *vierge*, a virgin oil. The tall, metal storage tanks, the *cuves* were more daunting, as it became apparent that a comprehensive tasting was obligatory. Thankful to be given the choice, we elected to use coffee spoons with which to assay the contents of each *cuve*, rather than the proffered alternative, cups. To some degree all such tastings involve an assessment of the worthiness of the potential client by the vendor. Happily, our comments must have indicated some intelligent appreciation, as thereafter we were allowed to buy some of the delicious oil, a small quantity only, and have succeeded in obtaining a small allocation in some of the years since. The reputation of La Balméenne is well-founded. The gorgeous translucent green-gold colour of their olive oil is accompanied by a degree of fruitiness and a depth of flavour that seems to us to be without equal.